THE ZEN OF DANCING IN THE RAIN

BECOMING ONE WITH THE STORM

AURITA MALDONADO

Copyright

CONTENTS

ACKNOWLEDGMENTS/ DEDICATION

This book is dedicated to those who feel that what society is expecting of them is not what they were born to do. It is for those who don't worship the religion of money, who are looking for proof that it is possible to choose a different path and live a meaningful life, connected with themselves and Mother Nature outside of a society where people would rather kill themselves than exist, even through the tragic moments that share space with the unparalleled beauty of being alive.

Serena, this book is for you. Lily and Angel, you, too. And of course, Oliver and Kayla. Choose your paths according to your inner compass. If you need support, call me. Remember, I was Uncle Bruno. As such, I could never do that to somebody else. I will not cut you out of my life. I will not discard you. I will not spread rumors about you. I will lift you. I will support you. You are valued and loved, no matter what paths you choose and where it takes you.

This book is for my babies, David Alexis and Auria Alexandra. You were created in love. You are love. And you are loved. I will support you with all of my heart no matter what path you choose, because that is the truest form of love. I accept you as you are. Completely. My Taino name is Niki Guarinara. Guardian of the Good Spirits. I am your guardian, not your master. You are not mine. People are not to be owned. You are yours, as are all of your decisions. I am here to protect and assist you, never to dissuade and discourage. To maintain open dialogue and kindness in my choice of words. You are already wise.

This book is for my soldiers and for those who have asked me how I do it after what we've been through. How I smile so quickly and easily after everything I've survived. I promised to write you something longer than a text message because the answer is important to me. I told you I was looking for a computer. I'm sorry I made you wait so long, Crystal, but here you go.

Here is your hope that there can be a fulfilling life after grief even in the brief calm waters between waves. Life during and after paralysis. Life during

2

and after war, loss, and abuse. Life after abandonment and familial judgment and banishment. Here's your hope that dreams do come true, when you listen to your intuition and follow the guidance you will find that you already know. Remember, you are the only one who knows your own thoughts. Be your own best friend. If not you, then who?

This is for those labeled crazy for not wanting to do what the masses do.

Own it.

If this is crazy, there's no way I'd choose sanity.

Healing takes work. Do the damn work.

THANK YOU first and foremost to my Dad. You set the example of acceptance for my choices. I feel your pride often. I imagine you and Alex spend lots of time up there or wherever you are interrupting each other and commenting excitedly about…everything.

Tammie & Steve Queen, Sue Arnold (**YOU BOUGHT THE FIRST COPY**), Julie & Randy Mladenoff, and Leroy Galloway: Your influences have shaped and molded me in the best of ways. I couldn't have asked for better role models to watch and follow. Seriously, you changed my life just by being unabashedly good human beings.

Titi Gloria, I know you see this from wherever you are. I feel your sarcastic ass smile. I love you. Hug my father for me.

Rosa Sosa, don't think I didn't notice you supporting and promoting me all of these years. I love you. Thank you.

Chipper, I love you. When this book takes off, I'm going to finally get you that wheelchair.

Knikki, you changed my life and continue to do so. I am forever grateful that I have had the opportunity to spend so much time with you.

Oscar, Sail Relief Team, and Finca de Hamberto – Solar electricity, a crib, food, animal care, transportation, a hot shower, a fellow combat veteran's ear, everything. I appreciate you.

Ricardo & Sandra (Picado y Sanna) You are the best neighbors ever. Thank you for helping during the hardest time of my life…You let me fill my water tanks at your house, lent me a car to make it to dance classes, and for "Café Ricardo," where I wrote part of this book!

The real heroes are the ones on this list. This is the list of those who had enough faith in my dream to purchase a copy before I'd even finished writing my manuscript to help me fund the production of this book. Thank you. Your support is noticed and appreciated.

One last shout out to my cousin, Christhie Gonzalez. They say that family members are the last to support business endeavors, but you went out of your way to mail me cash to order yours. Girl. Thank you. That is support.

Heather Obrien	Nicole Taylor	Sue Arnold
Cat Orr	Tiaya Ruggirello	Laura Phung Engle
Angel Vazquez	Henry Rivera	Claire M. Nelson
Anthony Howell	Lisa Young	Maria DeCicco Pena
Annie Nickum	Lilliam Shuman	Maryetta King
Christie Hicks	Thomas Turner	Deborah Maldonado Jaime Troche
Sarah Sidwell	Misty Lynne Sims	Liz Santiago Leith
Tina Ramirez	Karen Ames-Nocera	Roberta Sappington
Krystle Rose	Donnalise Wilson	Stephanie Freitag
Vincent Giammanco	Kim Chappell	Catalina Reyes
Alise Bifulk	Heidi Brinnich	Hiram Gonzales
Judith Marcus	Julie Mladenoff	E Lou Bjorgaard Probasco

Valerie Mowbray

Christine Fisher

Carrie Anne

Ariel (Jay) Colon

Meghan Kennard

Jasmine DeValois

Shannon Corona

Katrin Pantsosnic

Joanne Guerra

Ann Hobday

Venus Hernandez

Nicole Allen

Kat Stefano

Tammie Queen

Leroy Galloway

Chuck Collen

Rosa Sosa

David Rivera

Sharon Henry

Amy Helm

Amy Gordon

Kelley Curtis

Margarita Mendoza

Tracy Breidegam Dancause

Donald Poling

Dona Rodda Ramirez

Lindsay Anne

Laura Whitmire

Christhie Gonzalez Axel Coronado

Cathy Dickey

Lara M Gale

Courtney Shoecraft

Atira Rodriguez

Lita Haime

Emily Ad Kins

Szaritza Yamira V-B

Michelle Harline Rolls

Lorlee Wagner

Lupe Simpson

Kay Howe

Lisa Ghylin Paulson

Christopher Sievers

Amy Vitro

David Salai

David Hook

Amanda Musser

Jessica Mikenas

Serena Velez

Wendy Roberman

Carmen Erickson

Robert Bishop

Robin Williams

Emarae Garcia

Cathie Ambron

Erin Schrode

Tavonny Worlds

Alys Matthews

Lilliam Shuman

Angela Leilani Harris

Ann Tebbe

Rebecca Rivera

Fern Lozada-Rosario

Courtney Ryan

Kara Holmstead   Kathleen Graham   Joanna Gonzales

Liz Zivic   Ekom Enyong   Rachel Rowe

Stephanie Allen   Eliza LaRochelle   Alba Gonzales

Maryjo Seamon   Stephanie Allen   Diana Kapron

Rachel Duffy   David Sergienko   Lindsey Scranton

Melissa Drewry

INTRODUCTION

As a young child, I realized that I enjoyed each journey much more than its inevitable destination. The well-trodden path has never interested me nearly much as the overgrown, thorn-laden game trail. I often played a game with my friends called Hide and Seek Tag. To this day, I feel it's an excellent example of how I've chosen to live my life: while my friends trotted off to hide, I would instead use the time to run to the other side of my neighborhood as fast as I could. I would weave in and out of trailers, turn corners, and cut through well-manicured lawns. At a certain point, I would sprint at top speed back to the towering oak tree we called "base," and taunt whoever was "it" to chase me. I was grinning like a puppy that was just let out of the car and listening to my heartbeat pulsing in my temples. I loved playing a game with myself that allowed me to do what I wanted to do alone while still being semi-social with other children.

When we picked our characters to play "House," I always picked the dog. Even if there was an open spot for Dad or Mom, I wanted to be the dog. Dogs remain present and always in tune with the activity happening in front of their faces. They run to play, rolling in something because something smells good to them, smiling, sleeping in the sunny spot while everybody sits in the shade. That's what I wanted to be when I grew up. A dog. Living completely in the moment and running to feel my body move.

I enjoyed delayed gratification, and if a situation wasn't geared that way, I would create a way for it to be so. For example, I grew into a long-distance runner, turned marathon runner, and ultimately ultrarunner. 50 miles. While gaining experience training and racing, I realized that I truly loved the technical, rocky, dangerous courses that made me increase my turnover into quick choppy steps. They allowed me to express the agility and forced me entirely into the present moment to avoid injury. These terrains became a meditation for me - a singular focus. To increase speed in these areas is quite tricky, and without the proper experience, borders on stupid. As a result, most of these sections go much slower than the clear, open, grassy areas sans obstacles. Still, the footwork necessary to avoid a wrong step on the trail is a delicate dance that has continuously fed my spirit — a boogaloo with nature. Skip, change step, duck, slide right, *boom, clack, chick, taca-taca-taca.* Complicated syncopations are nearly marked in place, but progress, nonetheless. There is nothing except the trail and you.

The journeys in life can be this way, with easy flowering grassy knolls followed by deep, swift river crossings and rocky, technical strips through dense brush. During these times, it is necessary to slow your speed, quiet your mind, and focus entirely on the present moment to dance your way through the section without injury. You may even be able to take the increased rate of choppy steps with you into the next open section and push off with more pressure on the balls of your feet, thus increasing your speed even beyond that of when you entered without increasing your effort. Without fail, you will be grinning by the time you enter uninhabited terrain.

Forgive yourself quickly, every chance you get, even when it feels you are moving more slowly than desired. Not everything comes quickly, nor at the pace you choose. So be good to you, because each moment you live is the last time you get to live it. There are no do-overs, but don't forget that every second of every day is another opportunity to reset and start over. There is no statute of limitations to this. Age is not a factor.

CHAPTER 1:

A LOVE AFFAIR
WITH MOVEMENT

Before I entered the school system, my father was told that I would have a lot of energy, too much energy even, to have the ability to focus. He was advised to put me on medication to calm me down and keep me still. I am eternally grateful that he never listened. Instead, he took me outside each day. While he walked, I was allowed to burn energy running laps in Stoever's Dam, a family park with a shady 1.5 mile pathway that snakes through trees, encircling a large lake.

I loved the feeling of movement. If I was allowed to move enough throughout the day and find a reason to be interested in the topic being taught, I had very few problems focusing through school.

I ran to burn energy, compete, get faster, go harder and longer, but mostly I ran because I loved it. I would often catch myself wanting to skip when I walked. Sometimes, I would just feel the overwhelming urge to break into a trot and let out a scream of excitement for the blood coursing through my body. So, why not run? That burning feeling in my lungs, the feel of a torrential downpour of icy rain beating against my quickly numbing the skin, of the wind pushing against me, the burn of sweat sneaking its way behind my eyelids, not being able to speak through lips stiff with cold accompanied by the clear, intimate sound of my heart's methodical drumming in my ears feels like... unfiltered life. When the frigid air rushes from the world through my mouth, down my throat, and into my lungs, leaving them raw in its icy path, I feel the life in me erupt in pleasure. I become one with my body. In tune with every movement, each change in temperature, each effort. Suddenly, parts of my body that I rarely notice during other activities become major players. The way the chilled wind blows the soft hairs on my arms, the burning in my shins with each strike, the melody of my ventricles playing life's tune in step.

Becoming aware of these senses then searching to make them more pronounced drives my desire to run even harder. I feel pure life in making my own heart race. The awareness makes me smile, and the more "pain" I feel, the more my awareness grows, creating in me an overwhelming joy at being able to handle the burning sensation in my muscles. A joy that stretches my smile, often making me skip, yelp, or even break into uproarious laughter in appreciation of life. Moments of zen. That is when I feel the luckiest.

I feel blessed, almost guiltily, to have the ability to run, jump, dance, burn and reach muscle failure. Movement is a gift. Although it has been taken from so many, being conscious of this valuable gift of movement drives me to celebrate it as fully as possible for both myself and for those who aren't able.

I'm able.

Therefore I run.

In the 6th grade, I was a huge Civil War buff. I lived in Central Pennsylvania, about an hour outside of Gettysburg, read *Killer Angels* by Michael Shaara and watched reenactments with my class and family. I was young and in love with the romanticism of history. Death wasn't real. It wasn't a sudden and incomprehensibly final moment. It was like in the movies: romantic. A bunch of white men dressed in blue and gray shooting point-blank back and forth at each other over a big barren field. Most had bayonets fixed, and some stabbed at their opponents when they could get close enough. Every death was glorious and accompanied by a dramatic clutching of the chest while falling slowly and grunting loudly. When they weren't fighting, they stood by their clay cauldrons, cooking a fragrant chicken stew. I remember walking through their tent cities with my mouth-watering, looking on in awe as the grizzled men wiped the remnants of battle from their skin and wool uniforms. Death wasn't real, sudden, or final. It was solved with a bit of water and a paper towel.

It wasn't until I returned from war myself that I thought anything of those reenactments. The loss of life in battle is not pretty, glorious, or entertaining. Death cannot be solved with a bit of water and a paper towel. The remnants of battle remain, even if not physically; they remain in your mind, and they remain forever. A cruel awakening is the moment of realization and the shattering of childhood innocence.

I was a scholar/athlete in high school, but much to the chagrin of my teachers and coaches, I turned down a full scholarship to the University of Chicago where I had planned to study Political Science and International relations and chose to sign the dotted line for Uncle Sam on September 17, 2001, six solid days after 9/11. Even my recruiter begged me to change my mind when the towers fell, but he didn't know me well enough. He thought I'd be miserable and encouraged me to just drop the military mission and go to school instead. I understood how he felt.

School was fun and easy for me. I was 5th in my class and was already taking college courses after my basketball and track practices. Luckily, I'd had the opportunity to learn in a very black and white, undeniable way that my choices in life don't need to make sense to others. I had wanted to drop everything and play soccer my last year in high school but under peer and teacher pressure, I'd chosen cross country. Some of my teachers had challenged me and even bullied me for voicing my desire to do something drastically different, and I folded.

I ran cross country, the sport everyone knew I rocked, and I won...everything. I got the accolades, the medals, the hugs, and the high fives. Still, I was miserable because I felt like I was missing my opportunity to do what I wanted by doing what others had wanted for me because they were scared that I wouldn't receive enough playing time. I knew I wouldn't get playing time, but I'd wanted to train with them. I had wanted to play soccer the entire season, but I didn't claim the choice as my own. This time, when I felt the desire to join the military, that was what

I was going to do no matter who tried to bully me into making a different decision based on their own fear or lack of vision. Blame *G.I. Jane*.

Army Basic training was a breeze. I was already an athlete, albeit one with a quick temper and a smart mouth. I finished my time at Basic as the one private in my platoon chosen to be promoted at the end of the cycle. After that, I graduated from training at the Defense Language Institute for the Korean language with an associate's degree from Monterey Peninsula College and was quickly sent off to Ft. Hood and subsequently Iraq. I arrived at Fort Hood in early January of 2004 and had boots on the ground in Iraq two months later.

When my unit A co. 3 BSTB, 1 Cav Div. arrived in Kuwait to prepare for our tour in Iraq, our vehicles were not armored. It was really quite a mockery of the "American Dream." We were unprepared, and our best 50 Cal gunner had just been discharged from the Army for being a homosexual. After welding on heavy iron front doors, we departed for our three-day convoy from Kuwait to Baghdad. I was selected as a driver. Our trucks still had canvas back doors, and by the time we'd arrived in country, bullet holes decorated them like Christmas lights. Mortars, rocket and small arms fire, and Improvised Explosive Devices (IEDs), quickly became a daily occurrence in my life.

One night I was working on the top floor of a 6-story blown-out building in Baghdad we had deemed our office. At around 0300, I heard a loud *thump* on the roof directly above my head. When my shift ended, I went to the roof to check out what had happened. There was a completely intact 60mm mortar round. A dud.

Another morning, I was running 1-mile laps around the base with a scruffy, playful pup that ran with me regularly. As I neared a corner to cut behind a building that used to be a beautiful swimming pool, the pooch ran ahead. I felt the concussion of the explosion before I realized what had happened. A mortar had hit the path where I was headed and had killed my running partner.

A few days later, I was in a building that had been cleaned out for gym equipment when an explosion hit so hard that two mirrors came down from the wall. I ran outside to evade the collapse that was sure to come if the building had been directly hit. It hadn't. The ceiling did not drop.

I trotted quickly back to the "barracks" to check in, but on my way, found the source of the explosion. It had been a car bomb right outside of the compound's walls. There was a driver in the car when it exploded. How did I know? There was a charred, bloody arm in the middle of the road. It was not uncommon to pass burned, blown up vehicles on any mission, but to see it inside the walls wasn't something for which I was prepared. The smell of burnt hair and flesh lingers in my mind to this day. That smell never quite goes away.

When the time came for my mid-tour leave, I had the idea to surprise my father and stepmother. I gave him the wrong date for my arrival so I could show up at his door without him expecting anything. I called my mentor and friend, Tammie Queen, and she agreed to pick me up at the airport and help me surprise my family.

After several days of traveling in the same dirty uniform, I was ready to go into the house and shower. We arrived after dark. My parents didn't know I was coming. So, at 9 PM, when Tammie pulled up in her dark sedan, a soldier in uniform stepped out, approached the house, and rang the doorbell. They thought their worst nightmare had come true. I hadn't realized my miscalculation until my stepmother started hitting me and crying hysterically.

I'll never forget my father's face when he opened the door. His expression was one of terror and defeat suddenly turned to disbelief and then elation. He grabbed me suddenly, pulled me close, and held me tight. So tight that I could feel his heart beating frantically and his hot tears running down my neck. He thanked God. He didn't let go, and I awkwardly allowed my daddy to hold on until he was ready.

That time with my family was something I'll never forget. I went out to eat with my father and he couldn't stop bragging about me having returned from Iraq. I didn't place much value on it, and at that stage of my life, it even embarrassed me, but everyone around him seemed to be so impressed and happy to recognize it. He beamed. He was incredibly proud.

During my trip, I saw a boy waiting to cross the street at a crosswalk in Hummelstown, Pennsylvania. He was around 8-10 years old, with blonde hair and blue eyes. I watched him walk across the street casually, without a care in the world. He wasn't nervous about an explosion, car bomb, stray bullet, rocket, or mortar stealing his life. He showed absolutely no concern outside of being a child. I surprised myself as the sobs erupted. I needed to pull over. I felt incapable of driving without taking a moment to compose myself. That moment turned to 10 as I sat there for nearly a half-hour sobbing for the children in Iraq and the privilege of this American child who has no clue that his inherent safety is a privilege.

CHAPTER 2:

SALSA

When I returned to Iraq from mid tour leave, I got back into my routine of running every morning if I was inside the gate. My running partner happened to be the reenlistment NCO, and he joked with me often about coming to his office to reenlist. I didn't want to, and I said no. He asked and I said no, but I recognized deep in my deepest thoughts I was considering staying. What was my plan? I haven't finished my 4-year degree yet. I could finish it in the next enlistment and not doubt my decision to leave the second time around. What if I could go back to school for another 63-week language class? I love linguistics! I love school! Maybe I can learn another language, finish my bachelor's degree, and play in Monterey, California again! The more I thought about transitioning to civilian, the more I noticed that my answer wasn't

100% yes. I've learned that if it's not 100% yes, then it's usually my intuition screaming NO!

I walked into his office and sheepishly quipped, "So, if you could get me back to Monterey as a Mandarin Chinese linguist, I'd consider reenlisting..."

He laughed from deep in his belly, "Challenge accepted." The next day I was signing paperwork to return to Monterey, California to study Mandarin Chinese with a $15,000 signing bonus as a perk to the decision I'd already felt my soul requesting. I'd leave 6 months after redeploying to Ft. Hood.

When we returned from Iraq we deplaned in Dallas. The sides of the walkway in the airport were lined with supporters waving flags, clapping, and smiling. They shook our hands and thanked us for our service. There was a band. I remember thinking that it wouldn't have been this welcoming if I had been returning from Vietnam instead. I went back to Killeen, TX, and quickly picked up hobby after hobby. I found civilian society boring and needed ways to keep my mind busy. It just doesn't make sense to try to plug in when you return from combat. I got a puppy and hired a trainer to teach me to train him. I went rafting, hiking, running; I was constantly moving. Running races, 10 milers, half marathons, full marathons.

There was a "Salsa Night" on FOB Ironhorse in Iraq that I hadn't been able to attend, but I kept having this nagging feeling when I returned. If I could survive a year of war, what was stopping me from going dancing? If not now, then when? In the face of war, simple insecurity or lack of a partner didn't make sense as a restraint.

I searched for a place to dance. I brought a fellow Boricua female soldier with me, but by the end of the night, I realized we weren't there for the same reasons. She found more than a dance partner in someone and left with him to recreate the most primal of social dances in his bed. I went out one more time with her the following week, but then I chose to begin going alone. It was less of a hassle than having somebody drunk to babysit. I was hooked. However, during my first dance, my partner stopped dancing with me halfway through the song, and with a scornful look in his eye, asked where I was going. It was at that moment I understood that I was going to have to actually learn to dance salsa, not just go with, "*Claro que si*, it's in my blood. Of course, I dance salsa."

My reenlistment to study Chinese sent me back to the beautiful town of Monterey, California, and the Presidio of Monterey, and I was thrilled to go back to be "paid to go to school." I quickly realized that the

Chinese and Korean languages have some apparent similarities, like Italian and Spanish. I didn't need to study nearly as hard for the 63-week course of 6 hours a day language classes to keep up, and thus, had free time in the evenings to dance. In the beginning, the nearest big salsa nights and classes were in San Jose, an hour and 40 minutes from where I was living on Presidio of Monterey's joint service base. Every other Friday, I left Monterey to drive up to dance at 8 PM and arrived home at nearly 4 AM. I didn't drink. I didn't smoke. I danced, and danced, and danced. Soon, I began to go to the boardwalk in Santacruz on Sunday afternoons to dance at the "Salsa by the Sea" socials before returning to dance in Monterey a few hours later. When I found myself looking for things to do during the day on weekends, I purchased DVDs from instructors and trained alone at my house for hours every day before sometimes driving as far as San Francisco to dance at night. I popped in my language study CDs on the way and studied through the 3-hour drive. Sometimes I even brought flashcards with me.

It may seem like I sacrificed sleep, time, and money to dance. But, really, as long as I got my dance fix and still maintained a high GPA, I wasn't really concerned with how it happened. From my perspective, I didn't see it as making "sacrifices," I was making easy choices. Fair trades in time that enabled me to do what I wanted to do. I could stay in the barracks and watch television for 3 hours, or I could spend those 3 hours studying Chinese while driving to San Jose to dance my ass off. I could go to "The Duck" downtown and get drunk, or I could get dance high after dance high and remember the entire night with radiance. Eventually, I created an underground dance club, "Club Rita," in my own house on Monday nights. This led to some Tuesday mornings where I would disappear to change into my Army PT gear and head to 0515 Physical Training before the last person had even left the party.

I graduated from my Mandarin Chinese Course as the first in my class. I had earned an Associate's degree in the Korean language the first time I came through DLI. Now I had a solid number of credits in a second language and had been awarded the Provost Award for being the top of my class. One day towards the end of my class, my 1st Sergeant pulled me aside and asked if I would like to stay at the Presidio of Monterey as a Platoon Sergeant instead of moving back to Fort Hood for a second time. I accepted. It looked like I would finish my career in the Army there in Monterey, California, with only one tour in combat.

Meanwhile, what was happening in my personal life was a lot of downsizing. I had a 3-bedroom house and a husband when I arrived at Monterey. The Defense Language Institute is jokingly called the "Defenseless Love Institute" because of how many young soldiers, sailors, seamen, and Marines meet the "loves of their lives" and hastily marry, but then break up when the military sends each one to a different location. I hadn't entirely done just that, but almost. I married a quiet, intelligent Marine with a beautiful smile, a quick wit, who spoke Spanish and Italian and had a body-building hobby. We met in DLI in 2003 and stayed together through our assignments to different locations. In fact, we decided to be a "couple" the day after he left DLI and moved to Texas. Jacob and I went to Iraq simultaneously, but to completely different provinces.

We wrote to each other every day. Although sometimes our letters took weeks to arrive. We wrote numbers on each envelope, and when I returned from Iraq, I had just under 365 letters from him in my duffel. They included origami flowers he had learned to fold so he could surprise me with a bouquet and a sketch he had made of his favorite photo of me.

He moved with me to Ft. Hood after finishing his contract with the Marine Corps, and we stayed there for 6 months until we returned to Monterey, California together. He was the perfect take-home-to-mom material, and I loved his kind nature, but something inside of me had shifted. I was growing more and more dissatisfied with society and felt like I needed to be doing something significantly different. Several months after returning to Monterey for the Chinese program, he sat me down and told me that he felt like I didn't want to be married to him any longer, and he was right. We made a quick and peaceful exit from our nuptials, and although it was what I felt I needed to do, it broke my heart.

After we divorced, I moved from our 3-bedroom 2-bath house in Ft. Orde to a tiny one-bedroom one-bath cabin right next to the base with a large back yard and a beautiful garden in the front. All my personal items that no longer had a space in my home went into storage for the entire time I remained in Monterey. They were not missed. In fact, they were almost completely forgotten.

As a platoon sergeant, I found myself with much more free time than as a student, although I had just under 70 soldiers in my platoon. I had weeks of paid leave accrued because I hadn't even begun to think of taking a break that wasn't block leave, and during block leaves, I was only taking a few days around long weekends. One day, I was browsing for another race to run, daydreaming about traveling to a foreign land to stretch out my legs and lungs, when I saw a promotion for a stage race in Costa Rica, The Coastal Challenge. It was a 7-day camping adventure race over different terrains. Including a handful of adventures between races like white water rafting, abseiling, repelling down waterfalls, ziplining, a coffee tour, a bioluminescent swimming trip, and a trip up to the crater of a volcano. I felt a familiar tingle of excitement as I read the description of the race and decided that I needed to be part of it.

Every second of every day is an opportunity to choose to change your life.

I checked the dates on my calendar, and it seemed like it wouldn't be a problem, so I literally ran to my 1SG's office to bring it up with him. He had recently flat out denied my idea of a bicycle tour across Africa with some friends from Santa Cruz. Still, I thought that this idea to fly to Central America to run across Costa Rica was much more reserved. He checked the calendar and travel advisories, tasked me to write up a risk assessment for my trip, and much to my excitement, approved my request with only a handful of fatherly lectures about safety and operational security. Three weeks later, I found myself on a plane heading for an unknown adventure.

I didn't realize it was an anomaly to travel alone to an event like this until I arrived and saw that every single competitor had come with a partner. I won that race with a cumulative time 22 minutes faster than the next female competitor and returned to Monterey with a new zeal for adventure that broke the status quo. I had traveled alone and not only made a group of new friends out of strangers but also won first place and brought back plenty of fun stories. I met a race director who inspired me. He had created a race for himself, based on things he wanted to do, and I'd paid him to participate in his adventure. I had a clear example of a man who had a dream. Then he made it a reality in an unusual way. There were obvious hiccups with traveling across a country with racers in a beat-up van. There was a point where we were pushing it up the side of a volcano, but to me it was intoxicating the difference between this type of problem and the imagined issues of everyday life in the middle class US. Just like that, I was ruined for society's land of indoor offices and fluorescent lights. I spent every free moment I had daydreaming, plotting my next adventure, trying to recreate the powerful feeling of autonomy I had tasted in the jungles of Costa Rica. A place where my own desire to be there had fueled me. A desire to run, to dance in the evenings, and explore, nothing else. It was a pure love affair with movement.

I signed up to work on an Advanced Free Fall skydiving license to supplement my ever-growing need for adrenaline. I had seen a promotion for a discounted tandem jump, so I showed up. When I landed, I was screaming and hopping up and down (once I could stand up). What a high! I felt that nagging tingle of excitement that I've never been able to ignore. I went straight into the office and began asking about getting a license. It was an easy decision. I began to leave work every few days during my lunchtime to jump out of planes at 15,000 feet above sea level so I could finish my AFF basic course and earn the right to skydive alone. By the time a staff meeting would come around in the late afternoon, my adrenaline high was coming down, and I could barely hold my head up, but I was smiling all day long.

I began climbing, kayaking, and volunteering at the local Humane Society to pass the time in ways that inspired me. I signed up to go on every adventure I could find that interested me. I became the captain of the installation 10 miler team and trained capable female soldiers to compete in the largest 10-mile race in the world, the Army 10 Miler in Washington DC. We trained weekdays and Saturdays, rain or shine, sleet or hail, and I was always ready to run. Every morning I made sure to remind my runners how lucky we were to be getting paid to run in such a beautiful location. I've been a morning person my entire existence, leaping out of bed to brush my teeth, wash my face, and go for a run first thing with a giant smile. I could feel the positivity ooze as I chirped at them cheerfully while they stumbled sleepily to practice. I'm sure I got on some of their nerves.

I had been trained as a Sexual Victims Advocate, working with survivors of military and civilian sexual assault during the evenings that I wasn't spending dancing, reading, or running. After several months, my commander got orders to move on, and a different one took his place. This one was unhappily married and quickly let me know he had a crush on me and my "free spirit." I found myself in a dangerous position, as he had the rank and power to control my career, something he did due to my disinterest in his advances. One day, I decided to show the assault survivors I worked with that the "system" can work for you. I reported his advances with photos of text messages and emails he'd been sending me, along with all my rejections. I brought it to my 1SG, requesting that he intervene.

The system worked, kind of. My commander was given a letter of reprimand and lost his command, which is a stiff punishment as an officer. Most importantly, my phone wasn't buzzing, my email wasn't dinging, and I didn't feel his gaze lingering anymore. As it turned out, I wasn't the only soldier he was harassing. Several lower enlisted females had different photos of him fraternizing. He was sent to work in another office on the same post, but I would have to leave Monterey altogether.

I was told that I needed to leave the unit because anything the command there did with me could be misinterpreted. For example, if I got a positive review, one could think that it was because they were scared I'd report them. The same could be said for a negative review. The worry was that I could accuse them of retribution. I felt utterly betrayed, although I had to begrudgingly admit that it made sense. They lifted my "Fence" from my ideal position in Monterey, California as a mentor, running coach, and Chinese language tutor, which left me open to the needs of the Army. This means that the protection I had to remain in my position as a Platoon Sergeant and not get assigned to the first demand for my qualifications in a unit on their way to combat had disappeared. I knew

I'd be going directly back to war before my 1SG ever called me into his office to give me the news.

I was ordered to report to the 10th Mountain Division in upstate New York to take a team to Afghanistan. They were gearing up to deploy in 6 months. I was an E-6, a staff sergeant, and suddenly heading back to war again in a much different position than a lower enlisted E-4. I would be responsible for soldiers' lives this time around. It's a different beast to know exactly which decisions lead to a soldier's death in combat versus an ignorant blanket acceptance of soldiers dying in war.

Of the many things you learn in the military as you begin to rise in the ranks to Non Commissioned Officer (NCO), it is that you can disseminate tasks, not responsibility. There is nobody responsible for your duties, and all of your choices are your own to make, as are the consequences for those choices. If you have a duty and ask someone to cover it, and they don't show up, it comes down on you. If your alarm doesn't go off and you failed to set yourself a backup, it comes down on you. If you arrive late to formation because of traffic, it was your poor planning that got you there late.

The only acceptable response to, "SGT, why are you late?" is "No excuse" or "I failed to plan correctly."

35

You accept the consequence, because you knew the consequence when you chose the action. I had chosen to report my commander, and these were the consequences.

I had paperwork that told me a date to arrive in Watertown, NY, but I had no car. I'd flipped it on a drive to Texas two months prior. It was in this pivotal time of transition that I met DJ Skelton. This man changed my life in many ways. He showed me pictures of Alaska, and I felt the seed planted in my mind. I wanted to be there. He introduced me to Paulo Coehlo and showed me there was a different way to live, if I chose it. DJ offered to take me climbing one morning, and I jumped at the opportunity. We got an Alpine start, waking up hours before dawn to make the drive from Monterey to Yosemite. Our first climb was Lovers' Leap. While I sat perched on top of the rock overlooking the magnificent mountains of the Pacific, he asked me a simple yet life-changing question.

"How do you plan to get to Ft. Drum?"

"Well, I flipped my car on the way to Goodfellow AFB, so I have to fly," I answered matter of factly.

"Why don't you drive my car?" he offered it like it was normal to offer someone you just met a vehicle to drive more than 3,000 miles one way. "I have friends out there you can leave it with when you deploy to Afghanistan, and I'll have an excuse to take a road trip back to California!"

I looked at him hard, searching for a sign that he was joking, disbelieving, "I have almost a month I can use to get there if I leave in two weeks. But, your car, really?"

"Why not? I have two," he laughed, "I mean, she's a plastic Saturn and standard. I call her The Grape."

"I don't drive a stick."

"I'll teach you," he had a solution for every obstacle, "Say yes. I'll make you a list of places you must see along the way. I'll set you up with some climbing and running friends of mine. Go have an adventure." I felt that familiar tingle, a moment that I could make a decision and change my life. My soul had already agreed, and now I couldn't have it any other way.

So I did. I borrowed his car, he helped me create a music playlist to take with me, and he gave me a lesson on driving a standard car the afternoon before I left on my own. I took with me a map highlighted with different colored markers and notes, a GPS to cheat when I got lost, a camp stove, a french press, and a cooler full of meals that would save me money and sanity on the road, at least for the first few days.

Granted, this was my first-time crossing Colorado on I-70 through Aspen, Boulder, and I was nowhere near proficient at changing gears nor stopping on steep mountains, but that just added to the adventure.

The autonomy I'd felt in Costa Rica was nothing compared to the open road with my two terriers in the Grape. I stopped where I wanted, when I wanted, listened to what I wanted, and explored like it was my first time. Because it was. His mapped-out journey took me from California to New York through a network of incredibly scenic roads. I went climbing in Moab, Boulder, Colorado, and in the Gunks in upstate NY. I danced along the way. I slept in and around the Grape. I had a tent with me and two alarm terriers who would let me know if anyone or anything came close to me. I zig-zagged my way from California to New York on my own terms, but that taste of freedom really set me up for failure when I arrived in Fort Drum.

CHAPTER 3:

WE BLEED RED

I arrived at Ft. Drum in Watertown, NY in the second week of July. It was a shock to my system and to my peace I had found on the road. After 5 weeks on the road exploring, adventuring, running, and dancing, there I was, signing back into a new unit surrounded by downtrodden spirits without passion for their work. I still felt the sting of being sent away from Monterey, and arriving at a unit that appeared cohesive through shared misery already gearing up to deploy felt insulting. It lingered like the burning tingle of a hard slap in the face. The thought of being killed or, worse, maimed in combat before becoming a civilian just because my ex-commander couldn't stay professional infuriated me. I didn't believe in the mission, whatever it was supposed to be. "Winning hearts and minds."

I arrived and immediately moved into the living room of a tiny one-bedroom apartment that another soldier was "subletting" directly above a Chinese food restaurant. Yum. I had a faded red futon to sleep on and my bags, never fully unpacked, stacked in the corner. I had a sloppy pile of books I was reading, a laptop, and a few notebooks that I used to journal. Not much more. I never bothered to call the moving company to deliver my household goods because we only had a couple of months until we were deploying to Afghanistan.

On the other hand, I was on the east coast, only 3.5 hours to NYC and Philly salsa dancing. After living in the Grape for 5 weeks, crossing the country for fun, this was not an obstacle. It was an opportunity to hit the road and feel free and autonomous again. It was a way to find my sanity each week, make friends out of strangers, and share conversations without small talk.

Dancing can be some of the most intimate conversations over music. It can be the silliest, most playful, uplifting, enjoyably inspiring exchange of expression and connection if you allow that moment to exist and change your life. It is the body's most beautiful poetry.

I found myself leaving Watertown to dance every Friday after work. Just like in Monterey, if I was getting my dance fix, the method didn't matter. I brought podcasts with me to keep my Chinese fresh as well as comedy audiobooks and hit the road with my French press and cooler full of snacks. I brought a pillow, a blanket, and a book, and when the night of dancing was finished, I'd begin the drive to Annville, PA, where my father and stepmother were still living. When my adrenaline ran out, I'd find a place to park so I could sleep in the back seat for a few hours.

When I wasn't heading to NYC, NJ, or Pennsylvania to dance, I found myself driving to Syracuse, a scant 90-minute trip. There was a Cuban-style dance social in that area that I enjoyed attending. I taught ladies' styling, body movements, and social dancing. Both Watertown and Syracuse are in the lake effect snow region, receiving massive amounts throughout the winter. This proved to be quite dangerous in the Grape, but that element of the trip spoke to my adrenaline-seeking side. I distinctly remember spinning out, doing two 360's and facing the wrong direction of the oncoming traffic when she finally crawled to a stop.

I need to dance. Rain. Sleet. Snow. It is necessary. Often returning from the night in Syracuse at 3 AM, I found myself too tired to make the hour drive to Watertown without pulling over to take a nap. All the nasty gas station cappuccinos in the world paired with a side of even grosser energy drinks accompanied by the most upbeat music couldn't keep my eyes open after a full week of waking up for 10 miler training at 6 AM, followed by full days of work or training in the Secret Compartmentalized Information Facility, so I slept in the Grape somewhere in between.

During the days, my unit was preparing to ship out, which meant many field training exercises, trips to the range to zero and qualify with our weapons, last-minute workshops to learn new NSA programs in the Secret Compartmentalized Information Facility, and inventories. Lots of inventory checklists that had us spending many afternoons counting in the motor pool. I used my lunch breaks to run to the gym to work out. There was no airport close enough to jump from a plane, so I brought a book with me to each place so that I never needed to feel as if my time was being stolen while waiting for the next task.

The morning that we finally had orders to board the plane to Afghanistan was incredibly anti-climactic for me. We were to show up at the Company building at 0330 to head to a large gymnasium to do the last of the out-processing and farewells with our families before boarding a bus to the airport. I'd already become talented at compartmentalizing, so I spent the morning without really feeling anything but intrigue for my reading material. I'd brought a good book, a set of noise-canceling headphones, and set them up on the floor as we spent the day waiting for our bus trip to the airport to catch our flight to Kyrgyzstan. I noticed that most of the soldiers around me seemed to be with crying family members or lovers, but I had nobody to send me off that day. I felt hints of sadness whenever I'd look up from the book and glance around the room, seeing children sobbing for their mommies or daddies who were leaving, not knowing if it would be their last time seeing each other on this side of the veil. Lovers clinging to their last physical contact without knowing if their relationship would last or if their soldier would come back whole or in a box. Passively observing the storm for so many felt a bit like purgatory. There was no leaving the gym, no going to the city to dance, nor leaping from a plane to pass the afternoon, so I disappeared into the world I'd created in my imagination. The world of my book.

The process to deploy is quite time-consuming. You leave from the United States to a base in a different location to stage. When I went to Iraq, we stopped in Kuwait for weeks to prepare for our drive to Baghdad. This time, we were going to Kyrgyzstan. I deplaned, 18 hours after boarding. I remember being impressed by the mountains and immediately beginning to daydream about running and adventuring on their rugged terrain.

There is a saying in the military, "Hurry up and wait," and that's what we did. As soon as we finished preparing in Kyrgyzstan, we boarded the C130 to head to Bagram AirField. In Bagram, we prepped during the day, and then I would rush to the "Gym" and "Salsa Nights" at the hospital as often as I could in the 2-week period before our convoy to our real Forward Operating Base, FOB Airborne. I ended up splitting my deployment between FOB Airborne in Wardak, FOB Shank in Logar and rotating to each Combat Out Post (COP) in Wardak to train soldiers on the different equipment we were introducing for communications. I arrived at FOB Airborne a month before moving to FOB Shank, and for a few weeks, I was the only female on the entire base. The first female to live there in a full year.

I quickly met SFC Aldemar Burgos, a flamboyant Boricua, 2-87 Inf. Supply Sergeant. He always felt like a father to me, although he is only about 10 years older than I am. Puerto Ricans do that. We find each other no matter where we go. He was staying in the upper enlisted area, full of tiny furnished trailers we called chus. The higher up the chain you go, the better accommodations you get. I was put up in a tent with a cot. He offered me some *arroz con salchicha* that he was cooking over a fire outside of his chu. He told me a few stories, and we became brother and sister for life. We would meet at the chow hall tent to eat, and he would tell stories until everyone had left and the entire chow hall was cleaned. When it was built, his supply tent became the Boricua spot. We went to play dominoes, dance, eat, and watch movies. He was always willing to spend time with soldiers, always available to talk and laugh.

During a deployment to a combat zone, the military provides you with a 15-day mid-tour leave. They will purchase you a plane ticket to any location in the world (without travel restrictions) to have some rest and relaxation from combat. I felt like I needed an adventure, so I set out to pick a location for my leave. I settled on Ecuador, with its flora and fauna out of this world. One week before my mid-tour leave date, I left the Secret Compartmentalized Information Facility (SCIF) in FOB Shank, and as I sat in the break room I overheard some soldiers having a conversation that caught my attention.

They were making fun of another soldier for what they called "couch surfing." One explained the concept; people host you on their couch while you travel for free, and you exchange an experience in lieu of money. I was intrigued, a couch could be much more comfortable than the back seat of the Grape, and I was more than ready to travel again. The other soldier started laughing cynically and said that if PFC so-and-so was into it, he didn't want to have anything to do with it because "That guy's a weirdo, and who does that anyway? Sounds like some ax murderer type-ish."

I said nothing but the moment I got off my shift, I literally ran to the internet tent and signed in to wait for a computer so I could do a google search. Almost an hour of waiting later I signed in on a computer and found out all I needed to know. I was ready to be on leave already, and now I had a method. Over the week, I created a profile on the Couch Surfing website and began searching for hosts willing to accept me as an American soldier from Afghanistan with no references. This was in 2009, the early days of Facebook, and the entire world was not yet easily searchable by name.

I had an old friend, an exchange student from the Milton Hershey School named Sabastian that lived in Quito, the capital of Ecuador, with whom I'd planned on staying a day or so. I had 15 whole days to explore with nobody telling me anything about anything. I decided that I would only take one small backpack with a built-in hydration pack, one change of clothes, a pair of running shoes, a pair of flip flops, my laptop, my passport, and a giant smile. Two days before I left on my journey, my first host responded. He introduced himself as Wlady and said he'd love to host me. He told me that he owned land that included an animal sanctuary in the jungle and that he was heading that way to camp in a cabin he has there, take a group bird watching, hike, and swim in the river. He shared his goal of getting into eco-tourism and offered to pick me up at the bus station if I could figure out how to get to his town, Riobamba.

I arrived at the bus stop in downtown Riobamba at 2:30 AM after a 4-hour ride from Quito, and Wlady was there, just like he said he'd be. He took me directly to a large house and set me up in a bedroom of my own with a bed that was much more comfortable than a couch or the Grape's back seat. Around 8 AM the following day, everyone in the house woke up to a spread of bread, meats, and cheeses. I was surprised to see 5 more travelers had spent the night.

We went to the market and got on a bus for a few hours. I wasn't sure where we were going, but I was vibrating with excitement to be free again. We ended up deep in the jungle and far from society and any memory of Afghanistan for the first three days. Just where I'd wanted to be.Jumping into the river, visiting an orchid garden and animal sanctuary, hiking beautiful trails, bird watching, and eating and drinking well.

The next couch surfing host that responded was in Manta, the westernmost port of Ecuador. This woman told me that she wouldn't be hanging out with me, but I was more than welcome if I wanted to stay in her beach house on the water. She gave me an address to pick up the key, and that was it. I couldn't believe that trusting people existed.

Wlady emailed me again while I was in Manta and offered a horse trek to Salinas with a stop in some hot springs. I practiced saying yes. After I came down from the hot springs with Wlady's eco-tourism group, a couch surfing host in the Galapagos responded, so I caught a flight there and spent 3 days exploring one of the most amazing places I've ever been to. Blue-footed boobies, tortoises the size of ponies, and sea iguanas sunbathing everywhere. Santa Maria really is one of a kind. I was in love with my adventures. I had begun to adopt the mantra that "Strangers are just friends you haven't met yet," as opposed to the "I like dogs and horses, I tolerate people."

I noticed a few familiar faces in each town that I visited. Each tourist seemed to be taking a similar rotation around the country. One man easily caught my attention every time he was around. He was close to 6'4 with long bright red hair. A tall beacon of a traveler. I was having dinner in a restaurant one evening before going to dance when I saw him walk in with his group of friends. Towards the end of our meal, his group came over to our table to chat a little, like travelers often do. We gushed over our adventures and shared photos we'd taken at different beautiful locations and a little information about ourselves. He then told me something that would inspire me to make a decision and change my life.

When I asked him what he did for work, he told me he was a mountain guide in Alaska. My jaw dropped, my heart quickened, and through an intensely focused squint, I asked, "Wow, how did you get into that?" fully intending to then figure out a way to get into that myself. The thoughts would become words now. "I want to go to Alaska."

Once my deployment ended, my time in the service would be nearing its end, and it would be time for a career change. I had spent months researching returning to Monterey to attend the Monterey Institute of International Studies to study upper-level Chinese, but something was hanging heavily over that decision that I couldn't pinpoint. I was excited, but something was missing. It felt forced. I had the entire world open to me, and although I was interested in studying languages, the time didn't feel right.

The red headed traveler then explained that he had attended the National Outdoor Leadership School, NOLS, gotten his Wilderness First Responder certification, and the job came to him. I was shocked. At that point in my life, everyone I knew had been pushing a university education to such an extent that I hadn't even realized that there was such a thing as a National Outdoor Leadership School. I needed to know more. This would be my method to do what I wanted.

I realized that this beautiful experience was a vacation for me, not a lifestyle yet. I needed to return to war for the next 9 months, and that reality felt heavy. There was a smothering sadness sitting on my shoulders my entire trip back to Afghanistan, and even more so when I got off the plane. I had fallen hopelessly in love with traveling alone, hearing stories, and accepting universal guidance in allowing myself to be vulnerable. I had said "yes" over and over again to new opportunities, even if they scared me a little, and by the end of the day, I would always be surprised by the adventures that had unfolded due to my willingness to experience them without expectations. But now I was going back to war. I had resolved to find out as much about NOLS as I could and pick a direction to go with my life before I returned to New York at the end of the deployment. This time I was 100% sure that I was ready to move on, but I still felt like I needed to have something planned that stirred my soul to avoid any temptation of falling back into this abusive military relationship "one mo' 'gain."

The problem with having the resolve to do anything online when you are in a combat zone is... combat. Tragedies, KIAs, days of communication blackouts for family notifications, explosions, mortars, rockets, small arms fire, and long missions happen. I found myself climbing mountains overnight, spending nights in trucks that had overturned, manning checkpoints, carrying 60-80lbs of interception equipment, sleeping in blown-out buildings or out under the stars, or overseeing operations with low-level voice intercept teams wondering in the back of my mind how I could get paid to play in the mountains this beautiful without combat involved.

Searching women and children for weapons and explosives was something I found myself tasked to do often. On one of these missions we took control of a families' *qalat*, pushing all the family members to the enclosed front area to sit like dogs and wait while we used his roof as a command area for communications.

Qalat is the Arabic word for fortress or defensive position, but we used the word to describe every clay and brick dwelling. Their only crime was having a house that was conveniently situated for our mission. The men were told to crouch with their backs against the wall in an area where the goats relieved themselves, sit quietly, and keep their hands in sight. They complied as I was sent into a back room where 10 women hid from me behind veils until they were positive that I, too, was a woman. Even then, they hesitated to speak to me or make eye contact as I physically invaded their worlds, searching them for anything I deemed threatening.

The room was dimly lit and uncomfortably warm. It reeked of sour fear and stale sweat. I removed my protective glasses and Kevlar helmet and tried to comfort them with a soft voice and a smile, but nobody responded well to my very masculine presence in their world. I couldn't blame them.

Imagine a family reunion at your grandmother's house. It's 2:00 AM, and your grandparents, aunts, uncles, brothers, sisters, and children are all asleep when six men and a woman armed to the teeth run in, speaking loudly in a language you don't understand, pointing their weapons at you, and pointing you in different directions. Maybe one of them grabs your grandfather and guides him roughly out the front door. You are confused, scared, and wish for it all to stop. After what seems like an eternity, somebody that speaks your language is ushered in, and you are curtly informed that you are expected to wait in a room for hours with no cushions, just prayer rugs, while your father, husband, grandfather, brother, and eldest son sit in the mud outside. Your grandfather is getting a chill because he's still dressed in his bedclothes. A strange woman dressed in man's clothing comes into the small room and instructs you with poor language skills and bold hand gestures that she wants to see inside your bathrobe, but your baby is in your arms. She needs to make sure you're not hiding any weapons.

Feeling comfortable yet?

When I returned to the front yard, I was tasked with watching the men, holding them at gunpoint while they sat waiting on their haunches, backs against the wall. They spoke quietly among themselves and gestured slightly at me, they looked concerned. Finally, one of them startled me when he spoke up in a clear British accent.

"My father is thirsty. Would it be possible to have a drink of water?" he questioned politely. I was surprised and didn't answer his question right away.

Instead, I asked him where he had learned English. As I talked with Mohammed, another soldier filled a metal container with water and offered it to the young man. He smiled and graciously accepted the water we had been warned many times not to drink.

Mohammed explained that he spoke Mandarin Chinese, Russian, Spanish, English, Pasto, Dhari, and Urdu. At the same time, he poured the water into small clear plastic cups for his family. I responded in Chinese to test him. He explained that he had lived in Russia for two years, in China for a year and a half, and had learned English in Kabul at the university. He told me these things in Chinese. His tones and pronunciation were accurate as far as I could tell, and his vocabulary was impressive. I switched to Spanish to question his occupation. He, in turn, explained to me in more grammatically correct Spanish than my own that he was an interpreter for a Chinese construction company that was paving a road to access the Aynak copper reserves.

I switched back to English to ask him the obviously American question: "Why?" Why, with so many skill sets, with so much education, was this young, motivated man living in a mud hut in Akhund Khel as a farmer? Why was he sitting next to goat feces, drinking brown water, speaking with a US soldier that just took over his home? He looked directly into my eyes, and I saw a flash of mild amusement and disbelief but no hatred. His answer was simple.

"This is my home. My family lives here. Why would I want to leave?" This nearly knocked me down. I couldn't believe that I hadn't thought of that. The reality of war is ugly. The only real difference between this man and myself was where we were born. I was in his space. This was his home, obviously.

I felt my face burn. I smiled sheepishly and responded awkwardly, "Duh. Of course. Why did I even ask that?" We moved out before dawn, allowing the family of Afghans access to their home again. I had a deep gnawing feeling of sadness, dressed with waves of shame on the convoy back to the FOB while considering that family's night in the dirt, my assumptions, and my ignorance. I felt embarrassed for western society, for ethnocentrism, and for the version of me that existed the night before having that conversation. I met someone amazing, who could teach me many things: a man choosing to live in a mud hut. A linguist choosing to use his time to cultivate food for his family, not slaving away sitting idly behind a computer collecting money to then turn around and purchase the same food in a store that the government would tax. I met an equal, somebody who indeed bleeds red just like me. You only know what you know until you learn more.

CHAPTER 4:

IS THAT YOUR BLOOD?

It gets messy when you genuinely begin to understand that the people you are fighting against at war are precisely like you. Not every soldier signs up to be in the US military because of an overwhelming desire to kill for their country and protect your freedom. Some simply need college money, debt repayment, a steady paycheck, approval from someone in their life, an alternative to college, adventure, discipline, an alternative to jail, etc. The fine print is, while you may or may not get what you came for, you might get some time in war as well. That fact is the same for both sides. In Iraq, children were being used. Some were signing up because there was propaganda being passed around in leaflets stating that an American head was worth a lot of money. Some believed in the cause, while still others were forced. What do you do when an 8-year-old raises an AK-47 or a 9mm? Do you talk them down? Or do you kill or maim them? Surely there's another way. That hesitation you just felt is what they are counting on. In Afghanistan, it was the same.

War is ugly, simply ugly.

Towards the end of my deployment, I sat through a mission briefing that sounded like suicide. It went against all intelligence that we had gathered about a high-value target's location and placed us in a vulnerable, dangerous position. It was a mountainous region with spotty signals for communication, but "We have to do something" was the response received from all higher-ranking parties involved. My direct line supervisor was on leave, or I know he would have vetoed the entire thing as the S2OIC, the officer in charge of signals and human intelligence collection and analysis. Before I went out on this mission, I felt that there was a large possibility I would be killed so I had already told my family I loved them. We were a 30-man contingent and a tracking dog named Rico clearing an entire valley in Nerkh, on the valley floor. Obviously, we were being used as bait for intelligence, and it didn't look like it would end well.

The first night was uneventful. We were airdropped in the dark over a dusty field. Quick, easy, and anything but quiet. We only had our night-vision goggles and the light of the moon as we ran out down the ramp of the Chinook and fanned out quickly to set up security. We found a place to bunk down inside of an abandoned qalat, and quickly learned that communication (Comms) would be difficult. We were surrounded by mountains and PFC Andrulat was having trouble getting a signal out. Usually that means the mission doesn't happen, but "We have to do something, right?" So, we rotated pulling guard on the roof so everyone could get a couple hours of rest.

We were up before dawn collecting our gear and heading out on foot. It was meant to be a 4-day dismounted mission, deep in the valley, with an overwatching team of Pathfinders looking out for us on the ridgeline. What we didn't know was that the moment the Pathfinders had dismounted their Chinook, the first one out took a round in the head. KIA before they could even set up a security perimeter. They retrieved his body, remounted the bird, and evacuated.

We found ourselves in firefights early in the morning with extremely spotty communication for the rest of the day. The crackles of an AK-47 are distinctly different from those of an M2A2, and we were pinned down behind a wall hearing plenty of them. We laid down fire, waiting to move. The rounds cut into the clay wall inches in front of my face, followed by the sound every combat veteran knows instinctively, fingernails down tight pantyhose. Tzzzb. You never hear the round that kills you.

On each deployment, you have a group of soldiers who have gotten used to each other's company, jokes, quirks, and quotes. "Embrace the suck" is a common saying, meaning it's going to suck, so just embrace the situation that sucks as life and move on. As a result, soldiers tend to lean towards dark humor and music in combat, or so I've seen. This keeps your spirits high or often makes a snide mockery of them being low. In this case, we were singing *On a boat* by The Lonely Island Ft. T-Pain. Leaving momentary cover behind a wall that is being chewed apart by bullets meant for you is absolutely counter-intuitive, and so when given the signal to go, one would find herself screaming, *"F*CK LAND! I'M ON A BOAT MOTHER F*CKER!"* and the call of the next soldier comes, *"F*CK TREES! I CLIMB BUOYS MOTHER F*CKER!"* and you know you are brother and sister for the rest of your lives, be it seconds, minutes, hours, or many years.

Everyone made the move into the qalat successfully. We cleared it and positioned ourselves to defend it. Now, we had a chance to set up the radio and call back to the Battalion to request air support. There were too many of them, and we were pinned in place. We took turns, the mortar team responded, loud *thump* followed by an earth-shaking *BOOOOM!* A spatter of AK-47, then a joke or a song from one of us.

Eventually, the air support would arrive and blow everything up so we could move. We were bait, and we knew it. I had two mortars strapped to the back of my pack. Most of us did. It takes a team. It took us hours to move on from that qalat.

Later in the morning, we passed a qalat that took my breath away. The jagged peaks behind the qalat peaked through the open spaces used as doors and windows, and a young girl, maybe 8 or 10 years old, stood still, a splash of pink, observing us. I was in awe of the view. What caught my attention though was a boy looking at me with disdain, the only female in this group of male soldiers. I quickly pulled out my camera from my pocket and snapped a photo, so I could remember that moment. My first thought had been, "I wonder if he is going to try to kill me later."

We passed a large apple orchard on our way to search a small group of houses close by, and I thought, "If I were to try to kill us, I'd definitely do it from there." We arrived at our destination uneventfully and discovered that an elderly man had been knocked from his rooftop that morning by the concussion of a mortar. PFC Fowler, a young blue-eyed joker, did some first aid and assessed the gentleman's wounds. His shoulder had been dislocated.

Communications had been picked up that there was a three-pronged attack waiting for us on the road we had planned to use as an exfil, so we returned the same way we came, passing the same apple orchard. As soon as I saw the apple trees, I thought, "Yup, that's the place. I'd definitely kill us from in there," and noticed a man in all black clothing as I scanned trees. He had an AK-47 casually hanging from a three-point sling around his neck. I yelled out to CPT Jaunich what I saw. It is legal in Afghanistan to wear black clothing and hold an automatic weapon, and even if you're feeling edgy from being shot at all day, killing somebody without provocation is still a war crime.

Everyone halted. For what seemed like a 10th of a second, or maybe even 5 minutes, I looked into his eyes, and he looked into mine. Then he lifted his AK and fired.

At me.

I dropped in what CPT Jaunich later called a Superman leap into a tiny stream bed that didn't offer much cover and returned fire. We all did. He and his friends who joined him seconds after had the advantage of cover and concealment. We were completely exposed and needed to move fast.

We bounded our way up a hill, leaving young men in the orchard, wet crimson corpses covered in black, where living souls had been. Every step I took felt heavy, clumsy, and not quite fast enough. We finally reached the top of the hill, a decent distance from the orchard, set up security, and sat down as a unit to decompress before setting up to sleep for the night. It was at this moment that I pulled my bag from my shoulders and went to pull out a large bottle of raspberry iced tea I had mixed that morning. A sweet treat for myself after an intense day. When I pulled it out, the bottle was empty with pieces of black cloth inside and six holes. Three on each side. I froze, not comprehending. Just kind of staring blankly, disappointed in the absence of iced tea. I just wanted my drink. SPC Cody Carpenter was next to me. CPT Andrew Jaunich was on the other side.

"You've been shot," CPT Jaunich stated flatly, almost robotically, though it sounded to me like the words surprised even him, "Look, there are pieces of your bag inside the bottle." I broke eye contact and looked down.

I had been shot.

Three times.

Through my backpack.

Immediately the mood changed from "Let's decompress and set up a rotation for security" to "SSG MALDONADO'S BEEN SHOT! BLOOD SWEEP!" Hands were checking for wet blood. There wasn't any. The rounds had passed from one side of my bag to the other, missing my body and the two mortars tied to the back. I began to shake. I was visibly vibrating with chattering teeth.

"Wow. That was intense. Want a cigarette?" Offered CPT Jaunich, laughing nervously. I shook my head. "Want some Kool-aide? I know you don't smoke. That's all I have." I took the bottle and took a swig. There's nothing quite like the moment after close combat when you understand that you almost died or could have died. It's as if your life is palpable, nearly visible in its vibrance, and you can feel it like the pulse in your temples after sprinting up a flight of stairs.

I continued to shake the entire night. I repeatedly tried but could not coax myself to sleep. The day replayed every few seconds, and I found myself frequently, intentionally attempting to release the tension in my body. The tension, not only against that frigid October wind at 8,000 feet above sea level but

64

more so against my own racing thoughts, manifesting in my flexed diaphragm and chest. I was exhausted, but I was awake until I felt the urge to relieve myself grow uncomfortable as the sun began to crest the horizon. I walked away from my pack to gain a moment of privacy, but as soon as my trousers hit the top of my boots, the firefight broke out again. There was a bit of comic relief to being caught literally with my pants down. I laughed, cursing, as I quickly picked them up and retreated behind some stacked rocks, waiting for the calm before returning for my kevlar and weapon.

We were all in stages of undress, most having woken to the sound of small arms fire. I happened to have a camera in my pocket and took a short video of the fight since my weapon was out of reach. A moment after the *THMMMMP* of mortar fire, I found myself distracted by the rising sun.

It was indeed a beautiful morning, and I said it aloud, "Wow, beautiful sunrise," with the sound of automatic and semi-automatic gunfire as a backdrop. A juxtaposition of beauty and war as a blatant reflection of life. The next time we would draw fire was shortly after coming down from our overnight perch.

The rounds came fast, and again, we were without cover, left to run up an incredibly steep hill to distance ourselves from the shooters below. We dropped gear, dumped our packs on the trail, and continued with just our weapons and ammunition. My quads burned that beautiful fire that reminded me I was alive, but this time it felt like desperation. I wished for them to be faster. My legs were heavy. Leaden by days of combat that had taken a solid toll on my body. I gritted my teeth, driving my knees to the sky, trying to run faster up this hill, but the burn was holding them down. I felt like I was crawling slower than I'd ever run, and this time my life depended on it. When we succeeded in gaining ground, rounds began to rain down on us. We had run to escape the fire below and now were being shot at from somewhere above. We couldn't see who was firing on us, but their aim was close, and we were surrounded by tall cliffs.

Someone near me tossed a grenade, and our attacker's response was to increase their fire 10-fold. Now they knew that we didn't know their location. Each time rocks were kicked into my face by bullets impacting the ground in front of me, I found myself surprised to be uninjured. We were high crawling back down the hill, waiting for air support. My elbows and knees bled. PFC Carpenter and Rico, the German shepherd, were next to me one one side, PFC Andrulat on the other. I kept thinking the dog would be killed. Twice PFC Carpenter and I flinched at the same time. I glared at him wildly, and he returned my look. I thought the brass from his weapon must be hitting me, but that didn't make sense. I was on his right side, his brass spits to the left. We found out after the firefight ended, and we inspected the area, that we were flinching to incoming rounds that only missed us by inches. They had hit between our shoulders, kicking up dirt and rocks at both of us.

We spent close to 36 hours on that hill without being able to move. A medevac came and evac'd PFC Carpenter and Rico, who's paws were raw and bleeding. Then a bird flew in for a supply drop. We were getting low on ammunition. 2-87 Infantry Batallion HHC (Headquarters) was coming to support us down the hill with numbers, and we were waiting for them. We had air support circling the area every few hours to dissuade another onslaught.

It turned out that Command Sergeant Major (CSM) Spano was accompanying HHC (Headquarters) with my brother from another mother, SSG Bishop. The group showed up after dark, full of jokes, snacks, and worried looks for me, the only female on the mission. I had a middle finger prepared as a response. The

67

following morning we all made our way off the hill and walked hours to the Landing Zone to spend the night, clearing houses along the way. Our next task was to be airlifted to the ridgeline and replace the Pathfinders who had needed to evacuate and abort their mission on the first day. Somebody needed to perform the overwatch they had been tasked to do. Just like in any job, when life is lost, the priority goes to nothing more than filling the vacancy quickly.

We spent the night in an apple orchard next to the Landing Zone, and parted ways with HHC the next morning, heading by air to the same ridgeline where the Pathfinders had been attacked. We dismounted the chinook in the same location they had begun to dismount, cleared the area, and searched all the caves and tunnels. There were quite a few signs of contact. The Pathfinder's blood had not yet been eroded by rain and time.

When it was time to exfil, we were crossing a beautiful ridgeline, but a thunderstorm was rolling in and we were at 10,200 ft above sea level, so there was an urgency to our step. We were traveling with a Low Level Voice Intercept team, and the equipment that SPC Naber was carrying was beginning to shock him, preparing him for a lightning strike. The storm was coming fast, as was another dusk, and I began to feel the genuine danger was not an ambush by Afghans, but Mother Nature, so much stronger than any amount of human hate. We are insignificant. My body ached a steady dull throbbing pain, my knees and elbows were sore, and I had quite a hot spot on the small of my back and my trapezoids, where I was carrying the bulk of the weight of my pack. I hadn't slept in 6 days. The air was electrified, literally. The storm made our hairs rise from our arms and the backs of our necks. I was alive. The Pathfinder wasn't.

I thought of a young PFC I had just met a few weeks earlier. As we loaded him in the RG-33 Mine Resistant Amush Protected Vehicle (MRAP), I assured him that he was lucky to join the Counter IED team and that he'd have a good time. We sat shoulder to shoulder on the convoy. Two days later, his truck hit an IED on a mission, and when it flipped, he was crushed. He was the 50 Cal gunner sitting in the turret. I was alive. He wasn't.

When we reached the designated landing zone to return to the FOB, we were unsure if the mission would end that evening or if we needed to spend another night on the mountain with the impending storm. Logistics. After communicating with Battalion, it was decided that we would exfil that night.

We returned to the FOB on October 4th. 2 days later, I went out with the 10th group and Bravo Company for another mission in Akundakhel, but we never made it. Just before reaching the Durani bridge, we needed to pull over and search for the source of an overwhelming toxic smell that was burning our throats and nasal cavities. It took nearly an hour to locate and dispose of the lithium battery that had exploded in our truck. When we got back into the RG-33 MRAP and began to drive again, I put my boots on the edge of the seat across from me, but I thought of Command Sergeant Major Pat Corcoran, who had just broken his back in an IED explosion and adjusted my posture, putting my feet flat on the floor. I noticed that my weapon was unsecured, posing a threat to be a projectile if we hit an IED. The intelligence analyst in me thought, "We just stopped before the Durani bridge for over an hour. We are about to get blown up." I secured my weapon and looked forward through the windshield just as it happened.

200 lbs of homemade explosives ignited under the driver's seat of our RG-33, and we were flipping before there was ever a sound. 4.5 flips, over 200 feet. I opened my eyes to the medic yelling in my face, "Is that your blood?" Is that your blood?" What blood?

Huh? He was gesturing at my neck. I instinctively grabbed my neck, and yes, there was blood.

"I uh... I d-... I don't think so," I stuttered through my confusion and coughing fits. The smoke of the explosion was irritating my throat. It burned in an unnatural way, obviously scalded by the toxic chemicals we were inhaling. I tried to stand and saw SSG Bishop reach for me protectively as I fell. I tried again and felt a hand heavy on my shoulder.

"Stay down," the medic barked. I did, and after the sky finished spinning, it once more settled into its place above the horizon. He found the source of the blood on my neck and collar. The interpreter seated next to me in the truck had taken off his kevlar to adjust it just before the IED exploded, and head wounds bleed. A lot. A medevac was called for the driver and interpreter, but the rest of us were going to have to wait for support to arrive.

My right hand was swelling fast, and my thumb wasn't moving without extreme pain. I assumed I'd bruised or sprained a tendon in my hand holding onto the seat belt as we somersaulted across the desert.

Several hours later a Counter IED team would come to recover us and the vehicle. By this point, the adrenaline had already fallen, and we were back into the regular routine of pulling security and waiting. I was far away in another land reading a book, feeling sleepy, with my now useless right hand wrapped when our support arrived.

When I was spotted with the convoy, bandaged, conscious, and reading, there was clear disbelief, "SSG Maldonado! Again? You are either the luckiest or unluckiest f*cker I know. I haven't decided yet." We all laughed.

"Bro, I'm still alive. I'm lucky as f*ck." I quipped, smiling.

CHAPTER 5:

WAR & MOVEMENT

When I arrived at FOB Shank in Logar province, an impressive tent was designated as USO for recreation. I'd learned at that point that the best way to stay sane was to keep busy. Not just by filling a day with mundane tasks and sedentary binge-watching, but with things that ignite passion in one form or another and keep one interested in living, not just existing. Art, language, literature, dance, movement, fitness, animals, gardening, and nature are the things that speak to my soul in ways that even combat cannot mute.

In my first free moments on the FOB, I went to the USO to introduce myself as a salsa instructor and extend an offer for salsa classes. I made flyers and put them on the corkboard by the door and the chow hall. Everyone has to eat, and everyone has to check announcements. There was a lot of interest in my classes and dance social. I had soldiers and civilians of all ranks and nationalities come set their weapons down in the rack by the door and clear their minds of everything for an hour or so while focusing on learning to hold a deep Afro-Latin conversation without words. While dancing, tragedies and traumas stayed outside to allow laughter to enter the spaces created by movement, and we remembered to live authentically in that tent together, even if only for an hour or two.

When we were finished with salsa, a group of Nepalese men would come and dance, just to celebrate and share a taste of their culture with us. Their bhangra style leaps and bounces made one's knees ache to watch, but there was no looking away. They would hold their hands in a circle, their heads moving from side to side, forward and back, tilting this way and that as if separated from their necks. Their smiles were radiant, intoxicating, and contagious. They brought out a smile and appreciation for diversity so overwhelming that the ugly circumstances of our new friendship sloughed away like microscopic flakes of dead skin. These were honestly my favorite moments of salsa night. Each time I walked out of that tent, I left with a fresh, clean perspective and a new love affair with breathing and movement. The open door let the hot steam of movement dance into the frigid mountain air like smoke billowing from a campfire, making a last display of visible art as it filtered through the moonlight as the final ode to the fun we had inside.

I had a group of Czech soldiers with whom I was trading upper-level English lessons for beginner guitar and Czech lessons whenever our schedules aligned, which was usually two times a week. I used Family Guy episodes as a teaching tool to keep it fun and share a bit of humor about stereotypical American culture. I would watch the episode ahead of time and give them a list of what I thought were good vocabulary words and idiomatic phrases. The next day we were free; we'd go over the episode twice, the first time without stopping, the second breaking down each vocabulary word from the list. The focus it took to teach and learn left all war worries outside for the hour we were in class.

I was doing the same thing with a French soldier over breakfast. Each day I'd come towards the end of the meal armed with a French/English dictionary, and we'd sit and practice his basic English and my basic French for over an hour. I love languages, and the opportunity to practice with natives was something I couldn't pass up. I shared English lessons with Afghan, Czech, and French soldiers in exchange for some basic lessons in each language and left with friends. There was a young Afghan, who called himself Peter. He even brought me study material from Kabul to help me with my Pashto lessons.

I stayed at FOB Shank for nearly 5 months before heading with my Commanding Officer, CPT Sievers returned to FOB Airborne in Wardak province as the SIGINT (Signals Intelligence) NCOIC (Non-Commissioned Officer In Charge). My last 6 months of deployment would be spent between FOB Airborne and its surrounding Combat Out Posts (COPs) in the gorgeous, dangerous mountains of Wardak, 17 miles south of Kabul.

When I arrived back at FOB Airborne, the first thing I found out was that there was still no recreational tent to use to dance, but SFC Aldemar Burgos had prepared his supply tent to create something fun. He'd put plywood down to encourage my classes, and that's all I needed. I started teaching salsa lessons in his tent whenever a Friday rolled around and I wasn't on a mission. There was eventually a group of Boricuas who played dominoes in the back. He'd always try to make *arroz con gandules* or *arroz con salchicha* for the parties. A taste of authentic living through times of war. Sometimes our evenings would be disrupted by incoming rocket fire, but that was something to which we were accustomed and an easy trade for hours spent dancing to Frankie Ruiz with the aroma of *sazon* and *recao* lingering in the air.

Being the 4-25 Infantry Battalion Supply NCOIC, SFC Burgos was popular, to say the least. He would always surprise me with what he was able to "tactically acquire." There were days I'd enter the tent and be slapped in the face with mouth-watering aromas of *bifstec*, salmon, or lobster. Whenever I pressed about how he managed to get such good quality food, he'd always have this crooked little mischievous smile. His eyes laughed behind his glasses, "I have my ways, *ya tu sabes*! The kitchen staff loves me!"

Every day I was not on a mission, I ran, celebrating my existence through movement. The route I ran around the perimeter of FOB Airborne was just under a mile, and the loop I ran at FOB Shank was about a mile and a half that included a really fun hill. I ran loop after loop, keeping time with my watch, lap splits, negative splits. Feeling the life course through me, my heart beating in my temples. If I wasn't running, I was sitting on a stationary bike or the elliptical machine with a book and headphones. I could go anywhere I wanted in the world in those moments of fantasy. Sometimes I had running partners; most times, I ran alone. But, after my run, I would always end up in the gym for another hour of whatever muscle group I had scheduled to work that day.

When visiting COPs with no women, no gym machines, and not much circumference to run, I did cross fit. There was always a way to reach muscle failure. You can reach muscle failure with two 8 oz water bottles if you hold them long enough. The method didn't concern me, as long as I got to do what I wanted to do. My first-time visit to COP Blackhawk I met the SSG Bishop. I was to spend the night with Bravo Company feigning a checkpoint then climbing to an impressive ridgeline to oversee the next morning's mission with a Low-Level Voice Intercept (LLVI) team. He was far less than thrilled to see a woman attached to the mission, and he let me know immediately through his attitude and tone that he wished I had a penis.

I had already decided without seeing them in action that I had more endurance than at least 80% of the men on that mission, and so felt mildly amused at the sentiment that it would be me that couldn't keep up. It wasn't until dinner before heading out for the mission that the topic of running marathons came up and how I had qualified for the coveted Boston Marathon on my first try: the tough, hilly Big Sur Marathon course.

After that conversation, SSG Bishop began to look at me like I had a heartbeat.

We became fast friends for our quick, snide humor, and absolute obsession with movement. I soon found out that he danced tango, and I invited him to the Boricua spot to swap lessons. I'd teach him salsa, and he'd teach me tango. Anytime I heard that Bravo company was coming to FOB Airborne, I had a feeling similar to when as a child, my father told me my cousins were coming to visit from NY. It didn't matter what we were going to get into, we were going to have a good time and laugh the day away, even if it meant spending the day in the truck. The world was and remains a better place for me because he is in it, on this side of the dirt.

CHAPTER 6:

THE RICHEST WOMAN I KNOW

I returned to Ft. Drum with the torch team in the first redeployment of troops, and never saw SSG Bishop again in person. I had begun my paperwork to get out of the army (ETS) in Afghanistan, so I could hit the ground running upon my return. I wanted to become a civilian as soon as I possibly could, but he was going to reenlist and make a career out of it. He was going to be a LIFER. I'd joked with him that LIFER meant "Lazy Incompetent F*CK Expecting Retirement, though SSG Bishop is not lazy nor incompetent.

I got a basic apartment close to the post so that the moving company could bring me my household goods. I still had the same 3 bedrooms worth of nice furniture and things in storage that I had packed away during my divorce in 2007, three years prior. As

I looked at boxes upon boxes of vaguely familiar items whose absence in my life had not been noticed, I began to feel as if they were weight. A ball and chain for my leg and my life. Why did I need a 40-inch flat-screen television when I hadn't spent time watching tv for 3 years? Why would I invest in cable? Paying the electricity and water bill started to not make sense. If I was comfortable in the Grape, why did I own more? Why would I want more? If paying for these comforts meant I couldn't live in my style of comfort, I didn't want them. There are two ways to reach happiness with what you have:

- Use your time to work to have more (to then realize that there's no ceiling to your desires)
- Desire less

I had just spent a year with brilliant, linguistically superior farmers who were home and happy in simple mud and brick houses with satellite dishes on top. Dancing barefoot, celebrating culture with radiant smiles in a dusty tent. I began to think about the cost of storing my things while I traveled the world or moved into a van down by the river, which at the moment of my return from Afghanistan, was really my goal. A van is much larger than the Grape. $60 a month for 12 months is $720. That's akin to paying rent for things that I didn't want to live with in my own home. I couldn't wrap my mind around wanting to do that, but I had never been shown that it was possible to simply choose not to. Everyone in my family was following the status quo, working jobs they hate in order to take their 2 weeks of vacation every 63 weeks, including my father. My entire life he was changing professions to maintain his freedom while doing things he enjoyed, but now he was in a job that he complained about constantly. He had gone from fixing electronics and selling them after nursing school and working in hospitals. He printed and sold bumper stickers, photography, signs, business cards, even jewelry he'd made from electrical pieces and beanie babies. Living to sell things, he'd taught me to sell when I was only 4, but now he worked at PhilHaven, a home for the mentally ill as a counselor. I told him how I felt about things, and he offered to allow me to store them in the garage until I needed them. I tried to explain to him that I needed to get rid of them, but he didn't quite understand what I was trying to say. He swore I'd change my mind, so my 3-bedroom house full of stuff I didn't want went straight back onto the moving truck heading south on I-81 towards Annville, PA, minus the television. I gave that to one of the men from the moving company in New York.

I left Ft. Drum with my DD-214 in hand on the 12th of January 2010 and vowed I would do what I wanted to do, and that was that. In the past year, I had been:

- Blown up by a 200lb IED.
- Witnessed our supply truck being hit.
- Been shot through my backpack 3 times.
- Watched a French soldier get his jaw shot off by friendly fire.
- Told a young man he was lucky to change units two days before he was killed.
- Saw the whites of the eyes of a man as he tried to kill me.
- Spent weeks on missions outside of the FOB sleeping on the ground being shot at.
- Climbed onto the roof of the Tactical Operating Center to watch a meteor shower.
- Saw an incredible show culminating with an IED explosion outside of the gate.

If I didn't see a way to achieve what I wanted, I would find one because I had learned that, at least for me, living didn't come through ownership of things or sitting behind a desk for 8 hours a day in order to afford to pay for comforts I didn't desire. That felt like a passionless existence. I found life through doing things that made my heart beat faster. Money and living in a pretty box with Netflix didn't do that for me, movement and freedom to be outdoors did.

I was being offered work through my email inbox, text messages, and phone calls. Many of these were extremely well-paying positions with the Department of Defense or private contractors, but the trade would be minutes, hours, and/or years of my life doing something that I abhor for a cause in which I had no belief and, at times, absolutely loathed. My time would be wasted, and that felt unforgivable. I simply couldn't imagine wanting to live if I tried to rejoin the facade, winning the coveted air-conditioned office desk position behind a computer with an hour lunch break where I went to the same posh coffee shop every day, staring at my phone instead of talking with the people around me, listening to people complain that their coffee is too this or too that. These are the same people who would allow their entire day to be ruined by some spilled coffee on their white blouse in the morning.

That's why combat veterans cannot rejoin society. When you've seen the reality of war and life, society doesn't make sense any longer. It feels empty. A mundane farce. There are children aiming loaded weapons at slightly older foreign children who just took deep breaths and said silent prayers before breaking down doors with photos of their own children tucked in breast pockets. Their own children who are kneeling by their own beds behind secure doors on the other side of the world who pray to their God that He "Keeps Daddy safe while he fights to protect me and Mommy from the bad men." Kids being killed in front of their mothers, fire fights that last days, where the words, "Shoot anything that f*cking moves!" are screamed from hilltops while a grandfather is standing frozen in his field. Hoe in hand. Not daring to even look up from his tool. Yet Suzy's entire day was ruined because her order was mixed up at the coffee shop and she hit every red light on the way to the office, and oh my God what a frizzy hair day she's having.

I was often challenged by soldiers and civilians alike, "But, if you worked for (insert company) as security, flying Unmanned Aerial Vehicles (UAVs), or as an intelligence analyst for 2 years, you could travel the world for the rest of your life without working. You have a Top Secret/ Secret Compartmentalized Information government clearance! You're crazy not to take that job! Why not?"

What happens to my soul then? What happens if on day 364 of the year I spend hating life working for them, waking up with tears in my eyes for not following my heart, I leave the office and get hit by a truck while standing on the sidewalk? I would have to accept that I'd chosen to waste the entire last year of my life! Each moment is one I will never get to live again! Time is like water; it moves and flows constantly. Each moment that passes, passes for eternity. My heart says do it this way, so I will do it this way.

I defended my choices without hesitation, without second-guessing myself. I knew what I wanted to do, and I was going to do it because I already knew how desolate it felt to know I wasn't following my heart. I had the opportunity to take a moment to change my life completely, and their fear of the unknown wasn't going to deter me from what was calling my soul.

I sat through the transition briefings where an upper enlisted male, who obviously didn't feel passion for his job, attempted to intimidate those on the cusp of changing their lives into making rash decisions based on the "statistics" they present to support their message. "Remember, once you leave the Army, where you are taken care of by Uncle Sam (who loves you so very much), you will need to make this much to pay for rent, water, electricity, your car payment, car insurance, health insurance, property insurance, Starbucks, groceries, gas, phone, cable, internet, recreation, etc. Who could do that? It's difficult. You will fail. The Army is where you belong. We are the only ones who can make you complete. Don't go anywhere. We still love you. Here's a coin for your effort."

All I could think of was how ridiculous the message sounded when I was turning down six-figure jobs to apply to work as a river guide in Alaska, a job that paid $10 an hour, but would make me the richest woman I knew. A woman jumping at the opportunity to go to work, brimming with excitement for my job and my life. I was still anxiously awaiting their response to my application, but even if they didn't hire me, there was zero chance I would apply for a federal job. I had decided that if I wasn't hired I'd purchase a one way ticket to Central America and "figure it out." The vast majority of the expenses he'd mentioned were not only unnecessary for what I wanted for my life but also felt as if they would be more of a problem than a "perk." I would find my riches. The money follows the passion, not the other way around.

As I worked my way out of the military, I came to understand that I had returned from Afghanistan angrier than I had ever been. I had a shorter and shorter trigger to an explosion. I felt a simmer inside my body that felt frantic to get away from the mundane and all things concrete. I grew to despise the complaining, entitled attitude of everyone. How could they not see how dumb society is making them? I remember screaming at my father the day after I returned about how I wanted to have a drink at the bar up the street. He offered to go with me, but I had misinterpreted the offer as his need to protect me. The thought of him trying to protect me when I had just spent a year successfully protecting myself in the most horrific situations ignited a rage in me I had never experienced before. I passively watched myself as I exploded. It was a feeling that I couldn't explain once I calmed down. From the other side of events, it seemed to be an absolutely unreasonable reaction, and it left me exhausted and perplexed. That scared me.

CHAPTER 7:

TRAINING THE PUPPY: MY MIND

I had dreamed of going to Alaska, and now my thoughts, words, and actions were aligning. That is the most beautiful feeling there is. Instead of entering society to hate my lack of courage to do what inspired me, I had been hired by the rafting company to which I'd applied in Haines, Alaska, and was gearing up to take a 6-week road trip to get there for the March 7th show date. I reached out to couch surfers and friends in every area I planned to visit, including Lake Tahoe, where I would stay 10 days to get my Wilderness First Responder (WFR) certification. I removed the back seats to my RAV4 and set up a sleeping pad. I packed a camp stove, a couple of jars of propane, my French press, and enough food for the first few weeks. I had more clothes than I would need and excitement I could barely contain to hit the road.

During these days, I began to notice my thoughts drifting to topics that involved anger, hate, jealousy, and a steady disdain for things that didn't go exactly my way or follow my way of thinking. I'd daydream while running and find myself angrily running through lists of things that irritated me about people and society. I didn't like those thoughts, but they kept returning, and when I'd sit down to write about them later, they evaded me like a butterfly teasing a kitten. I thought if I could capture those thoughts, I could understand myself better and like myself more, and that's what interested me. I wanted to become my best friend, as I realized I was the only one that truly knew these thoughts. I needed to be my biggest, most beautiful project if I wanted to be present and authentic. I'd tried a therapist, but all she seemed to want to do was hug and cuddle me like a wilted flower. I wasn't even close to wilting. I'm not even a flower but a fierce Ceiba, enraged. She had never seen combat, and I couldn't seem to understand why I was paired up with her. I decided to stop going after my first visit and settled on a voice recorder and a decision to get to know myself as a beautiful, powerful, inspiring woman more than I'd ever been interested in learning about some random handsome man. I settled on a voice recorder that would be easily manageable, 4 inches long and two inches thick, so I could hold it while running.

I made myself a promise that I wouldn't censor anything I was going to say like I had found myself doing in the past. The fact that someone could read my journals caused me to censor some honest, ugly thoughts that I truly needed to explore. I would make the best effort to pay attention to the second voice in my head that tells the first to shut up, just in case. Armed with my voice recorder in my center console, a Kbar 12-inch knife under my seat (in case a mother-f*cker would), everything I needed to survive in the back, and my two Jack Russell terriers, I set out for Alaska to change my life.

Six weeks later, I arrived in Haines with hours of recordings of me huffing and puffing, musing, and running all over the United States and western Canada while I communed with Mother Nature through movement. I found running and talking to myself hugely cathartic, and I still hadn't even listened to any of the recordings. Just knowing I had recorded it felt like progress because it was progress.

Haines is a breathtakingly beautiful small South-East Alaskan town nestled between the Takshanuk and

Chilkat mountain ranges with a bustling population of 2,500. It is situated at the northern end of the Lynn Canal, the longest and deepest fjord in North America. They say that you don't need to use your turn signal in a town like that because everyone already knows where you are going. Everyone but me. When I arrived, I knew I was supposed to go to guide housing for Chilkat Guides LTD, but I didn't know where that was. I was going to be working on the Chilkat Bald Eagle Preserve, 48,000 acres of protected land that includes the Chilkat, Kleheni, and Tsirku rivers. A chunk of land that can be visited by more than 4,000 bald eagles during the winter season and that remains home to moose, bears, wolves, otters, swans, and beavers year-round. All 5 classifications of pacific salmon travel up these rivers to spawn. I was going to change my life in a big way. I walked into the first bar I saw to grab a quick bite and a drink before asking for directions. The Pioneer Bar (P Bar). I began chatting with an energized blonde who was sitting at the bar. Alisa Beske. It turned out she was going to the same place.

After the first night of living in guide housing with my fellow workers and manager, I knew I'd need a more private place. I went out to hear some live music at The P Bar, The Fish Pickers were playing were playing energetic bluegrass. I stayed seated at the bar, watching what seemed like the entire town pile into the tiny room and begin to jump around without a single insecurity. I was mesmerized. It didn't seem to matter to anyone how they were dancing, or if it was to the rhythm of the music. I had never seen anything like it. They were moving because their spirits told them to, and that was it. I fell in love with Haines, Alaska that night. Everyone was welcoming, and it was that night that I was told of a "very rustic cabin" towards Chilkoot Lake that sounded perfect for me. It had been built upon 12 Sitka Spruce tree trunks and floated at super high tide. Over the last 50 years or so, 3 of the 12 tree trunks had drifted away and left one side of the cabin dangling precariously over the ocean. When I saw the cabin, it was love at first sight. 10 miles out of town, I had no neighbors except the RV park about 300 meters away and Jim Wilson up the hill. My closest neighbors were three brown bears, Speedy, and her two cubs, that came to visit daily. I felt my soul filling with riches like never before.

The cabin came equipped with a propane camp stove, a wood-burning stove, and a sink connected to the nearby freshwater spring. There was a faded green couch by the door. A separate bedroom with a few boards nailed into the wall led through a crawl space to a loft furnished with a mattress and a tiny triangle window to watch the tide. There was no electricity, cable, water, heat, insurance, internet, or car payment to pay, and the rent was $400 for the entire season, not per month. There was minimal phone reception, so I forced myself away from technology and into the moment. Here and now. Not then or there. I hung my own pictures on the wall. I had a collage of photos from Afghanistan, Ecuador, California, the Galapagos Islands, and my road trips across the United States. I had them to remind myself to be thankful every day that I'd had the opportunity to visit such beautiful places and that I was no longer in war. My recreation came in the form of running or biking the 10 miles into town, floating down rivers, watching nature from my porch, a kayak, fishing rod or net, and meeting travelers on the eagle preserve.

Soon, I was getting paid to do my dream job in my dream location. That was my recreation! I was ready to hit the ground running, literally and figuratively. I was already beginning to ask about offering salsa classes on my first few days. I found the arts center, where I heard there was a Neuromuscular Integrative Action (NIA) class that evening with Knikki Cinnoco. I had never heard of anything like it, but the description I read on the flier said it was a blend of martial arts, healing arts, dance, and spiritual self-healing. Anything dance related, I'm there. I showed up and began the class just like any other new class I've taken. Listen to the instructor and try to follow instructions. The class began easily enough, and we danced around the room in a fun, connected manner throughout the hour. The problem that I had was during the cool down.

Knikki took us through a relaxing routine to calm and cool down our bodies, and when she got us to the final instruction to relax the tension in our necks, I complied. I exhaled, felt my body loosen the last of its tension, and suddenly I was inside a truck being blown up, a flash of the whites of a young man's eyes, the flash of a muzzle. I flinched to dive into the streambed. The sensations were absolute, and my eyes shot open as I dropped defensively, ready to return fire. My heart raced. I felt it echoing in my temples. I glanced around the room. Everyone was relaxed. Heads hung limply. Knikki was following her own instructions and deep in her own body. I alone had that moment of absolute panic. I realized that I was breathing erratically and began to control my breathing. Focusing on my breathing gave me the break I needed to let go of the terror and remind my body that I was in an exercise dance class in Alaska, not Afghanistan. That was the first time I'd ever experienced an attack like that, but the next was only a couple of days away.

Part of the guide training we were being offered as new Chilkat Guides was a body awareness/yoga/warmup type activity with a powerful woman named Maggie. I followed her instructions, but I hesitated and considered holding the tension when it was time to relax my neck. I felt terrified, but I felt that to beat it, I had to control it, so it was necessary to understand it from more than one angle, which meant I needed to allow myself to experience it repeatedly. I swallowed, took in a deep breath, released the last of the tension, and broke out of the peaceful moment with a sprinting heart and frantic breathing again, followed by free-flowing tears. I knew I was in Alaska. It didn't make sense.

I was still on my mission to run and talk to myself until it all made sense, and that continued, day after day, mile after mile. Some days I'd run back from the 19-mile takeout (19 miles out of town) to grab my bike in town and continue the last 10 miles to my chilly little cabin. I began listening to my recordings and transcribing them to understand them differently. When I finished transcribing them, I printed them out to read them, with a bright yellow highlighter at the ready. As I read through my rambling, excited, angry, happy, hurt, satisfied, jealous, kind, racist, sexist, beautiful, and ugly thoughts, every time I involuntarily cringed at something I'd written, I hit it with the highlighter. Anything that I didn't want somebody to know about me, I made sure it had a mark.

Then I wrote essays on each of them, delving into the why or how, but as a third-party observer, without judgment, just interest. Like a new mother watches her baby with wonder, learning who they are through observation. I was my own science experiment, my own work of art, my own dance. I began to realize through this process that I could be any style of human I chose to put in the time to become if I understood where I was in my recovery and why I was there. I needed to be my own best friend, not my worst critic, and I wanted to be. That was the true beginning of a crucial transformation of perspective.

Over time, the NIA instructor, Knikki Cinocco, and I grew a close friendship that I value dearly. It was she who shared a piece of wisdom that changed how I looked at the world completely.

She said, "You know, it's not about worrying about other people judging or what they think. It's about learning not to judge others about anything. If you really pay that much attention to your own judgments and correct yourself when it happens, you'll realize you make so many that you don't have time to worry about what anyone thinks because it all stems from one's own insecurity." I took what she said and decided I would take that task on like marathon training, without fail. I paid attention to my own judgments, no matter how slight, and each time worked to kindly shift my thoughts immediately to accept a person's choice as their own. I treated myself as I treat dogs while training them. You give a positive reinforcement for the action you desire, and a simple negation for when they don't do the correct task. You don't scream or beat them. Degrade nor force their faces into their mess. That only breeds fear of you as the trainer. You give them the negation word and repeat the exercise again and again. And again. Calmly. Until they learn. The more I understood how many judgments I was making and why, the more it made room for grace for myself and everyone around me. I began to recognize behavior patterns in others that I now clearly realized I had mirrored in my own way.

Now my runs took a different tune. If I made the judgment, I corrected myself but talked out where the inspiration to do so came from and why that was an insecurity. I needed to understand, and I felt like I was beginning to get a decent grasp of who I was. I started sitting in silence by the water, listening to the sounds of Mother Nature, She who absolutely withholds judgment. In the beginning, I would stay with my eyes closed, focused on being a sightless observer of her art for a pre-set time. Five, ten, thirty minutes. I'd set an alarm and find myself startled out of a completely beautiful meditation. Eventually, I got rid of the alarm and sat until I was finished. Often for more than an hour. I wonder about the doctor who recommended to my father to put me on medication to calm me down and make me sit still. I wonder if he'd considered meditation before overwhelming a child's body with chemicals.

CHAPTER 8:

THE PEACEFUL WARRIOR

The sitting still, the runs, the writing, and the recording were fantastic. I was radiating positivity. But, as I found peace throughout the day, I found Hell beginning to arise at night while I slept, where I hadn't even begun to touch the tip of the iceberg in guiding my thought patterns.

The ground hurts my elbows. I'm pretty sure the last time I went down, they were cut on the sharp edges of rocks. I backpedal quickly, trying to ignore the stinging and dull throb, but at the same time wanting to give into it, curl up, and go to sleep. My knees hurt as well. My eyes feel grainy. There's smoke, or is it dust? I see a spark a few feet in front of my face. A second later, a sharp sound. Louder than I expected. Closer than I expected. A zipper. Then another. I duck my head. At that moment, the realization comes. If I'm hit, I won't hear a warning.

It's up to fate whether the next one ricochets towards me or not. If so, will it ricochet low enough to get under the brim of my Kevlar? I crawl back a little faster. Digging my elbows into the shale-covered dust to gain speed. I'm sure by now they are lacking skin entirely. I'm aware of every ounce of myself. I feel a bead of perspiration escape from the confines of my Kevlar, hastily snake down the front of my ear, onto my jawline, down the side of my neck, and finally, disappear again into the collar of my dusty shirt. Each time I shift my body backward, my shirt rides a little higher on my torso, exposing my belly to the hot grains of sand and sharp rocks. Every movement I make feels exaggerated. My clothes are soaked, clingy. I pull once with my index finger, my trigger finger. I'm not even sure what I'm aiming for. I pull again and again and again. Where are the shots coming from? Is my cheek even against my buttstock?

Another spark. 10 inches this time. I fire back. Round for round. I'm scared to look up. If they are above us, there's no way out. If I raise my head any further, a round is sure to squeeze through. Would I even feel it? Or would I just be gone? What if it hits the top of my Kevlar? Would it knock me unconscious?

I desperately want to be on the big, cushy green couch at my parents' house in Annville, Pennsylvania.

Curled up in a nice thick wool blanket with my terriers, sipping warm, sweet chai with milk and cinnamon that my mom has prepared, and watching a movie. Any movie would suffice, really. It could be about the most mundane or entertaining subject, just as long as it didn't involve me being here on this hill. I'm not sure why I'm here. Someone told me to go, and I'm returning fire. That I understand. If I don't shoot back, I will be killed. But WHY am I here to begin with? Why are there people who want me dead? And why is their aim so accurate?

Without warning, the inside of my shoulder is on fire. It's as if a thousand tiny red-hot knives are stabbing me from the inside, ripping and scalding muscle and flesh along the way. At once, I drop my rifle and grab my shoulder. My hand is wet with blood. I press down to suffocate the flames, but there are none, just the smell of burning alive. The men to my left and right seem not to notice me. I'm screaming frantically for their attention. I reach for my tourniquet. It's in a small pocket by my right ankle. Things are continuing loudly around me, but I sense that nobody can see me writhing in pain in the dirt. My hip hurts. I'm in the fetal position. I can't work the tourniquet. I can barely even hold it. I focus entirely on the operation of my fingers, trying to move first my index, then my thumb. My right hand is numb, my left is shaking. Then I realize I can't tourniquet that part of my shoulder. There's no way to stop the bleeding.

The cold, sudden realization that I'm going to die makes me retreat into myself. I no longer try to call out for help. They are busy anyway. Everyone is returning fire. The incessant cackling of M4s and M249s is deafening. My ears are ringing. I'm sure I just heard a grenade, followed by another barrage of rounds from the Afghans. Or was it from us? Nobody has communication with Battalion back at the FOB. Nobody had time to set up the sat phone, so there's no way we could get a Medevac, even if somebody did realize I was dying there, next to them. It doesn't matter anyway. The guy who's supposed to be manning the radio is probably waddling his way to the chow hall to get a fresh hot chocolate while I'm coming to terms with moving on to the next stage in life, whatever that may be. I can't help but think back on my decisions in life. How have I ended up here, of all places? Finishing 5th in my class in high school, turning down a full ride to the University of Chicago, a decision to join the Army after 9/11, language training in Korean and Chinese, two deployments, a whole lot of dance, and finally, volunteering for a mission in Afghanistan that would end my life.

Before I went out on this mission, I knew that I would be killed. I had already told my family I loved them. It was a ridiculous mission. I began to get angry thinking about it. I was bleeding out while the guy who came up with this genius mission was sipping his mocha, nice and warm in his cushy office, concerned only with watching the latest pirated episodes of True Blood on his laptop in surround sound. I watched him buy new speakers the week prior from the Hajji Shop. I was bleeding to death while he worried about what Suki Stackhouse might do next with Vampire Bill.

Finally, somebody noticed me, just as I started to fade. PFC Fowler's face creates shadows on mine, blocking the harsh sun for just a moment. His eyes flash, and I see the whites of the eyes of a man in black and a muzzle flash before things go completely black.

I would wake up with cold, clammy skin, my chest rising and falling without control, panicked. Every single time. The nightmares weren't what happened; they were versions of what could have happened embedded within real events. In one, I bleed out from my shoulder. In the other, I have a flesh wound in my arm, but I bleed out through my hip, and in the third, I shoot PFC Cody Carpenter in the back when I flash him with my muzzle while high crawling backward, away from fire.

On Memorial Day, I called Merlin Quiles, my closest friend. He was a Sapper from 2-87 Infantry, part of the team that came to get us from the hill where we were pinned down, and part of the team that recovered my vehicle when we got blown up. I confided in him that I wasn't doing well. I told him about the nightmares. The fear of sleep. I explained what I was doing during my runs to become the kind of person I'd rather be and my love affair with nature, but I couldn't figure out what to do about the dreams. I found myself scared to fall asleep, making excuses, reading all night, campfires, parties, drinking myself to sleep.

He told me that he wasn't having problems like that because he was following the instructions his therapist had given him. She had told him to talk about it all day long, but then at a certain hour of the evening, he would dedicate his time to something soothing and positive. I later found out that he wasn't doing any of what he had told me, but at the time, it was exactly what I needed to hear. I began to share bits and pieces of information about myself to my rafting clients and was surprised at their excitement to hear more. I shared my thoughts on war if they asked, I answered their questions as honestly as I could. I maneuvered around the emotions and anger it brought to the forefront of my mind when I touched the topics because that's unacceptable in the service industry. Sometimes they knew I had a purple heart when they chose my boat, sometimes they never found out, but in one way or another, I spoke it out every single day, on a mission to heal.

One day I was at a potluck on Mud Bay. I found myself answering questions, explaining to a gentleman why I always run with that little black stick, talking to myself. He wanted to know about my nightmares, my problems, my combat. He was intrigued. He then told me that he was Tom Morphet, the newspaper director, and wanted to do a story on me. The following week, I saw my face clearly looking out from someone's back pocket as I ran past them on the sidewalk. I stopped at the Mountain Market to pick up a copy, and there, on the front page, was the headline "Wounded Vet Runs to Shake Trauma of Iraq/Afghanistan." I felt my face flush as I looked up from the Chilkat Valley News. I felt like the entire store was looking at me with a different expression, and I couldn't quite place it.

The newspaper in Haines is published once a week, so I was on the paper's front page for an entire seven days in this tiny mountain town of 2,500 people. Flying under the radar was not going to happen any longer. If it had even for a moment. There were many reactions of surprise. Some folks changed their entire way of being around me as if I was an armed explosive. I went from being a fun, crazy hair, salsa dancing, river guide to an intriguing, dangerous female wounded vet overnight.

When my guiding season ended, I had another opportunity to do anything in the world, so I flew to Spain to participate in the largest food fight in the world. 14,000 people throwing 25,000 lbs of rotten tomatoes. I had wanted to do it since I was a child, and this was the first time I had the freedom to do so without the Army, my high school, or my parents telling me no. So at 27, I went to the tiny town of Buñol, Spain, and couch surfed with a combat-wounded Spanish soldier who is now my brother for life.

When I left Spain, I spent three weeks in Maui. I visited my stepsister, Rosa, and got to know Maui enough to decide to come back soon. We grew up together since I was 6 years old. I applied for a scholarship to the Boulder Outdoor Survival School and was awarded a free 28-day field course for the essay I wrote explaining why I wanted to leave society after seeing the reality of war and become an extreme minimalist. So, for 28 days in September, I was in the wilderness of Boulder, Utah, being taught that what I had thought encompassed becoming a minimalist wasn't even scratching the surface.

I was still running, recording, transcribing, highlighting, and trying to figure out how to handle PTSD, nightmares, and rogue angry, violent thoughts. I began to take the essays I had written for my own understanding to open mic nights. There is a single-screen movie theater and coffee shop in Annville, Pennsylvania, that I frequented almost every day. I took the thoughts that I wanted nobody to know about, those that plagued my subconscious, and I read them in front of an audience on Monday nights.

The sharing was difficult. I burned red, reading my own sacred words that I'd not censored for approval. I read them, and at times I cried. Most times, I laughed nervously, but every single time I shared, there would be a large group of listeners, artists, or just folks who'd happened by who would come to my table afterward and thank me for being brave enough to say things that they'd thought but never dared to say. This was the most liberating of everything I had done for myself to that point in terms of healing.

Courage is a funny concept to me. It's not really a thing like the destination isn't really a thing. It's not a lack of fear. It is packing that fear and taking it with you while doing the task anyway. It's screaming at the top of your lungs, "F*ck land, I'm on a boat, motherf*cker!" while you run as fast as you can to throw yourself into the doorway of a qalat under fire. It's taking your most private, ugliest thoughts, dissecting them, taking a deep breath, and displaying them for the world to see. All the things you'd hide at all costs, throwing them out into the world to see, and realizing through this that we are actually not very different at all. Only through doing that, releasing the exclusivity of knowledge, did I reach a place of freedom from the insecurities guiding those thoughts. Then the anger could slip away.

By the time I had returned to Alaska for my second year of guiding, I had a whirlwind of new lessons and experiences. I was teaching salsa at the Chilkat Center, running more than ever, couch surfing every opportunity possible simply to share stories and culture, meditating, and feeling like I was winning the battle. I had cultivated the patience to listen (I use the word cultivate because that's what you do with skills like that, you work on them until you grow the result you want, just like planting a garden). Anyone who needed to talk had an ear with me. I felt like I had a completely perpetual source of energy to lend or donate because mine was not finite. I was not in war;

therefore, there was no empty cup. I focused on giving to give, and only when I wanted to give, without expecting anything from anyone, and I was never disappointed. Anything can be spun into a positive without expectations. I didn't mind being told things I already knew because there's always a chance to learn new information from a different perspective. I allowed people the freedom to talk about anything. Anytime a friend of mine seemed stressed, I'd extend an invitation into my world to perhaps provide a series of peaceful moments through their storm. I had a few take me up on the offers. They later shared with me what a life-changing experience it had been to sit on my porch watching big brown bears fishing for salmon while eagles circled above.

I felt as if I was really getting a hold of not judging anyone for anything. Acceptance was a huge goal of mine, and I felt satisfied with my progress. I still wasn't sleeping incredibly well. I still had nightmares. I still shot PFC Carpenter and bled out regularly in my bed, but I awoke in the morning with renewed gratitude that those moments were behind me and only haunting me in my dreams and sporadically during the day. I ran marathons and did crossfit whenever I had a chance to clear my mind. I liked to run up Mt. Rapinsky, a beautiful mountain in the Takshanuk mountain range with Knikki. She would hike, and I would run the 3,000ft to the summit. I'd run ahead, hit a spot, double back to where she was hiking, then run ahead again. She never judged me for needing to move more quickly and double back several times, and I never judged her not wanting to run. She was my best friend in Alaska, and I was learning all sorts of new ways to be patient through her light, flighty, friendly presence. She didn't like to commit to a schedule in any way and could easily begin an adventure three hours later than the agreed time. By choosing to spend time together, I learned the value of making plans and entertaining myself with something productive until they began. Hurry up and wait, but don't waste your time being irritated about waiting. Those are moments of your life you will never get to live again, so find something positive to do with your mind.

Intentionally cultivate peace.

I was ready to accept peace into my life. I finally got rid of the last piece of jewelry I'd brought back from war and replaced it with a peace sign. I had a rule that the second time any of my jewelry broke, it was time for a change. The second time this particular piece of jewelry broke was in the middle of a Zumba routine I was dancing in the pavilion for the South-East Alaska State Fair. I felt it snap as I leapt into the air and clapped my hands, but I didn't care to look down until I'd finished the entire routine in absolute ecstasy. When I saw which bracelet hit the ground, I was stunned into silence. It was the last piece of jewelry I had brought back with me from Afghanistan. I had just purchased a beautiful bone carved peace sign from a vendor before Zumba had begun. I had danced to these songs with it bouncing around my neck. The clarity of the message raised my head. I felt myself checking for spectators, obviously somebody else would have witnessed something so incredibly profound. Everyone around me was smiling. The excitement still lingered from our dance, but nobody had noticed that my last physical souvenir from war I had kept with me for so many months had fallen and been replaced by my clear intentions for peace.

It was clear that the bracelet had served its purpose and would allow me to set the angst of war down to fill its space with calm, and I began to give myself permission to do that. Months later Donna Catotti, a local portraiture artist, painted a portrait of me wearing only that necklace and named it *The Peaceful Warrior*.

I felt as if I was on my way to achieving my lofty goals of managing PTSD in a classy, peaceful way through running, movement, rafting, and dance. I had managed to stay single for a solid two years of beautiful moments and gratitude. I casually declined every offer of courtship from all sexes. I felt I had reached a form of Zen in a reciprocating love affair with myself, life, and Mother Nature. Dancing with my traumas as a present, intuitive follower. I felt enlightened, powerful, capable, and calm. As is the weather before the storm.

CHAPTER 9:

A DANCE WITH DEATH

As I was getting ready to head to the lower 48 for guiding off-season, my boss at Chilkat Guides, Andy Hedden, sent me an application link for a reality TV adventure race because he felt the show's description looked like they were asking for me, specifically. I took the opportunity to make a funny video, write a few essays, and eventually received notice that I was chosen for a face-to-face interview in LA. They paid for my flight to LA from Haines, Alaska, for the weekend. What a culture shock. When I walked into the interview, the first thing the casting director told me was that I was the kind of person they were looking for. He didn't ask me any real questions. I was in and out in less than 5 minutes. On the afternoon of the 29th of August 2012, I received word that I had been accepted and would be catching a flight to Fiji in five weeks. They sent a packing list and told me they'd be in touch with an itinerary once they purchased the flights.

I would have been jumping with excitement, but I read this news through swollen, sandpaper eyes. That morning I received a call from my stepmother, sobbing. My father had taken his own life. My first love. My hero. The man who chose to keep me out of the system at seven months old by raising me after my birth mother abandoned my 3 older siblings and me for nearly a month in an apartment in Lebanon, PA, had parked at work and shot himself in the head in his car. He was a therapist at PhilHaven, a mental institution. My dad, who jumped at the opportunity to go to court to fight for custody and won by default because my mother never even showed up, left his brains on the headrest of his little red Toyota.

The news shattered me, and once again, I was with Knikki Cinnoco. The third year in a row. I had met up with her to have a latte at Sara J's when I received the call before going inside. Knikki saw me take the call and instinctively approached my side as I responded to my stepmother in a straight, matter-of-fact tone of absolute denial and careful disbelief, "No, he didn't."

"Yes, he did," she sobbed, "He shot himself in the head. We had an argument on Monday. I said I wanted a divorce. We didn't speak for 2 days, and today he shot himself in the head at work."

"Okay. I have to go," I said calmly, robotically, "Thanks for the call. Yeah...." I trailed off as I hung up. Knikki caught me as my knees buckled, and I sobbed into her shoulder the news I'd just received. My dad was the only person in the world that I never had to wonder about being proud of everything I'd done. Even my choice to turn down a full ride to school and join the military. My daddy was gone. The man who chose me when my mother discarded me. My hero. My first love. The man who printed out everything that I wrote and brought it with him to work to read to anybody who would listen. He'd left a basic, generic poem he'd copied from the internet with my name written on it before exercising his choice to move to the next adventure. In his defense, it was an innocent way of looking at things. He probably thought the poem was Earth-shattering and beautiful.

I was crushed and confused. I had driven into town for our coffee date, but Knikki didn't trust me to drive myself back to my cabin. Honestly, neither did I. I had walked into two parked cars and couldn't find a solid equilibrium. I was scheduled to work that day, and my old friend Jason Chambers was to arrive later that morning from New Jersey to make some life-changing memories for himself. Knikki took me to the office after she called and gave my manager the news. I wasn't going to be working that day. I asked to have a raft set aside to float on the river, even though I wouldn't be on shift. They said yes.

Everything about that day was a blatant example of how tragedy and beauty can share the same breath. The sky was cloudless, and the river was enchanting as always. The Cathedral Peaks remained, and the eagles continued their hunt for salmon. I, alone, was shattered on that river. I was with two people in the raft, though completely alone with my thoughts. I recognized that I was in paradise, surrounded by breathtaking views that hadn't been dimmed in the least by the death of my father. We are so insignificant.

I eddied the raft to walk around a bit. The tears had begun to fall freely, and I wanted to feel free to scream. I did. I screamed at the top of my lungs. I skipped rocks and screamed in torment, pain, hate, love, and pleasure. I screamed until my belly was cramped, and I had to relax and take a breath. I screamed until I was out of scream. I felt a moment of hollowness. Light but empty. The void they'd left behind quickly filled with the crisp afternoon wind and wild smell of boreal rainforest. Alaska. That's when it was okay to get back on the boat. I managed a slight smile, though my eyes involuntarily closed as my lips curled. I was tired.

My father's suicide left me with a desire to heal the world even more than the debt I felt to society when I returned from war. I wanted to be kinder to everyone than I had ever been. I quietly challenged every conversation I'd had with him, searching them for clues that it had really been my fault that he didn't want to play the game anymore on this side of the veil. At the same time, I stretched my imagination in an attempt to completely accept his decision as having nothing to do with me. It is his right, and one of the only ones we truly own, to take one's own life. Since returning from Afghanistan, I have been vocal about those feelings that choosing when you die is the only true control we can take over our lives.

The Universe has a funny way of challenging all beliefs you hold true. Six days later, I was looking at my father's frail, hollow corpse. Waxy, shiny with makeup, and tiny. I said an awkward goodbye with my stepmother standing in the room and turned away from the empty shell of the man who had chosen to raise me and subsequently had chosen to move to the next phase. I could feel that his soul had already left, I imagine before his intestines were removed. A short while later, I was solemnly handed a black box, heavier than it looked, that radiated heat. It was almost too hot to hold comfortably.

I saw the fire's effects on his skin in the cremator vividly in my mind. The blue flames ignited on the chemical-laden makeup until I realized it was time to turn off my imagination and focus on the real here and now. Even thinking about his skin burning felt less painful than the real here and now. I clutched that small black box in the garage of the house my father had shared with my stepmother. I hugged the box to my chest. Eyes closed, tears silently streaming down my cheeks. I felt him comfort me with his warmth one last time as the room bustled with people who had already arrived to celebrate his life. It was time to let go, but I wasn't ready. I didn't want to.

As promised, five weeks later, I was sitting on an airplane on my way to Fiji to participate in *72 Hours*, the reality adventure race that would air on TNT. Teams of three would jump from a helicopter into a river and navigate their way over 3 days to a chest of $100,000. The first team to make it would win the money. We were given a GPS that read direction and distance to each checkpoint, marked by a bright orange flag, without topography. The challenge was navigating the jungle. River crossings and land features made walking a direct line impossible.

I learned a lot about the production of reality tv shows in watching the final product. They created characters that they felt fit us and stuck with them. The show never mentioned that I was a veteran, nor did they include anything I did while we were in the jungle on the survival side, aside from navigation. They portrayed me as a peace-loving, wild-haired Alaskan river guide and nothing more. Not offensive, just grossly incomplete. I was told by the crew that I was being too calm in all the "emergency" situations that weren't true emergencies. If nothing is in serious jeopardy: life, limb, or eyesight, there is no emergency. Maybe if I had really only been the peace-loving river guide, they would have felt more intense, but not to a combat veteran cultivating a peaceful existence, who lives for adventures in Mother Nature.

They attempted to antagonize and low-key insult us when in situations they deemed as possibly explosive...Explosive for someone who hadn't really experienced an explosion. Strong reactions sell, I guess, but my initial response was to giggle each time it happened. Lighthearted giggling in the face of very safe adversity doesn't sell. I was regularly met with a contemptuous, "We can't use that... You're not giving us good TV."

My team didn't win, but I definitely took something home with me on the flight to LA from Fiji. Since it was the day after this adventure, "72 Hours" racing through the jungle that actually lasted 96 hours, I should have been tired, and I was, but I couldn't sleep. When it was time to get off the plane, I felt weakness and heaviness in my legs that I attributed to the race, all the while knowing it was something more. I had a sensation of being bitten inside of my body, and it kept startling me. I felt as if I had chills from being sick, but not in my core, in my extremities. I decided that I must have a parasite from the river water I'd inevitably swallowed, the slug I'd ingested, or the puddle I rested in during the race. I struggled to stand in the customs line, feeling it necessary to lean without a wall nearby. Waiting to get through customs felt like a bigger challenge than the entire race in Fiji.

After I made it through, a plan to go climbing for two weeks needed to be rescheduled due to my inability to sleep with the pinching, itching spasms that plagued me the entire night in my Rav4. It had grown worse than on the flight. I was positive I had a parasite. It felt like I was being eaten alive from the inside out throughout my body, and I was weak, exhausted, and shaky. A coordinated attack to challenge my sanity. I would slap and grab at my skin, expecting to feel something, but it was just my skin.

I decided to go to my mentor, Tammie Queen's house in Phoenix, only 4 hours from Joshua Tree, where we had planned to go climbing. We arrived at the doorstep of the woman who has been the kindest motherlike figure I've had in my life, and she opened them wide. I told her that I needed to go to the emergency room the next morning.

When I woke up, I had trouble walking. My legs weren't responding as they should. The right one seemed to be doing better than the left. The sick chills had worsened, my back hurt to sit up, my head hurt to lift, my neck felt stiff and painful like the day after a nasty accident, and I hadn't defecated in several days, but when I got to the Phoenix VA Healthcare Center, it took a solid four hours to be seen in the emergency room. I was sent home shortly thereafter with some Ibuprofen and treatment for a UTI. I tried to explain that I had been in Fiji and had to have parasites, but that wasn't considered in their lack of diagnosis.

What they did consider was my status as an out-of-state combat-wounded veteran and my emaciated condition. They noted my invisible pain and inability to move without screaming and spasming as well as the lack of evidence of a medical problem in my urine sample. They didn't search for more because what they did find in my urine was THC. So, they grabbed the gateway drug propaganda from the 80's and 90's and labeled me a detoxing addict looking for pain medication. They sent me away.

Six more times over the next three weeks, I would visit the emergency rooms of two different hospitals in Phoenix: West Valley Hospital and the Phoenix Veterans' Association Healthcare System (VA). The second time I came to the VA, it took 4.5 hours in the waiting room, screaming and mewling in pain before I took the effort to lay down on the floor to ease the torture in my back. The moment my back hit the floor and got my feet up on the seat of the wheelchair, I had nurses lifting me, scolding me. A veteran had died recently while waiting to be seen in their emergency room. He had been thought sleeping, and it was no longer permitted for anyone to lay down on the floor. Immediately, I was brought to the back and given a bed.

I wasn't defecating or urinating easily, and it hurt. My belly was distended, and when urine finally did come out, it was as if the drops were lava lined with razors. I whimpered and sweat profusely during the process. 7 days had passed without evacuating my bowels before they finally did an X-ray and saw that my intestines were backed-up full of fecal matter. So much so that my other organs looked like they were squeezed into the top corners of the picture. My entire torso was literally full of sh*t. They had to give me three enemas to clean me out the first time, flushing saline into my colon through a tube stuck up my butt. That time they sent me home with a diagnosis of constipation and a bag of enemas and laxatives because "treat the symptoms," not "find the cause." I was progressively losing weight. The 5th time I went to the hospital, they sent me home with the simple diagnosis of "dehydration" because, although I was losing consciousness and hallucinating in the emergency room, once they gave me a few bags of saline, my mind cleared a bit, and I was able to hold a coherent conversation.

I was dying. I knew it, but nobody seemed to have an answer for me. The sensation I felt was invisible, a burning electrical short in my system that was overwhelmingly painful all the time, without a moment's rest. My skin had grown sensitive to light, leaving me sobbing and screaming under the burn of fluorescent light. The closer the light of a flashlight was held to my skin, the more desperate I was to get away, only without the ability to move. I'd lost my reflexes, my equilibrium, and was short of breath just trying to speak. When I could speak, I'd get lost in a myriad of vocabulary, sometimes completely missing every part of the sentence except the nouns. If I wanted somebody to scratch my head, all I could spit out was, "T-t-top." A linguist without words. How ironic. The thoughts were in my mind clearly, but I was having serious trouble expressing myself.

Infuriating.

My body felt as if it had been made of powdered nerve endings. A light breeze had me whimpering. The sensation it left as it brushed against my skin felt like the same fire my father's corpse had endured. Nobody could touch me without causing me stabbing pain. Millions of red hot needles, like an iron brand whenever anything touched my skin. Having somebody sit on my bed changed the position of the covers and the way they rested against my legs. It made me grit my teeth, sometimes blacking out from utter torture. I had the gray hue of death's approach to my skin, but I was still being turned away in the emergency room as a drug addict.

Just a month before, I had taken a fast 20-mile run for fun, and now not only could I not stand on my own, but I also lacked the ability to comb my own hair, turn my head, empty my bladder, brush my teeth, lift my own fork, wipe my own behind, or even speak clearly. I spent hours lying on the floor in the shower. Focusing on the hot water pelting my skin with my feet flat against the wall was the only position in which I could find a slight reprieve from the pain. Getting up from that position was impossible on my own and an expensive payment in extreme pain.

The sixth time I went to the hospital, Tammie said, "Steve and I are going with you, and we are going to stay here until they admit you." That day there didn't need to be a standoff because somebody listened. The doctor decided that I needed to see an infectious disease specialist. The hospital I was at did not have one, but the Phoenix VA Health Care System did. She wrote a referral, and the next day we returned to the VA hospital to finally get me admitted.

When the infectious disease doctor saw me for the first time, he was livid, "This woman is dying! How has she not been admitted?" Just like that, I was whisked away to intensive/urgent care as an inpatient. After a series of tests, they found nothing, but I had a glucose level of 27. They didn't understand. I should have been dead. I had mentioned to them that I was in Fiji, and I'd ingested a slug just like I'd mentioned to every other doctor and nurse along the way. After a short while, during which I assume they searched Google, I was taken for a spinal tap. Almost two complete vials of cloudy, gray liquid that should have been clear was pulled from my spinal column. It was sent to the CDC for testing, but the doctor told me that the results would be delayed because it was Veterans' Day weekend. How ironic that the combat-wounded veteran could die Veterans' Day weekend because the CDC is low on staff and too busy celebrating the holiday to rush an emergency spinal tap. He said that he was fairly certain that I had gotten eosinophilic meningitis from the parasite, angiostrongylus cantonensis "rat lungworm," but without the results from the spinal tap, he couldn't know for sure. He spent hours fighting on the phone with the CDC, to no avail. I would not be getting test results in any reasonable time frame for the shape I was in.

He asked me if he had permission to treat me for rat lungworm without the test results. I agreed. However, he'd also asked me in the same vein if I knew what the spinal tap was, and I responded, "Of course, you stuck a big sword in my back." I was floating between consciousness; I felt my dream world fusing into reality.

A dance with Death.

Each doctor tried to judge my state of mind by asking me simple questions, and I was getting them grossly incorrect. For questions like who won the election and what day of the week it is, I had a decent excuse being in a near coma sleeping 20 of the 24 hours each day for the previous 3 weeks.

Before I went in to receive the treatment, I remember my doctor explaining to me in the hallway that there was a 50% chance I'd wake up from this, but also a 50% chance that the medication that kills the parasites could then cause an infection my body might not be able to fight off. I distinctly remember feeling no emotion about it. I was dying. Why not try something to change that. But at the same time, if dying takes away this horrid pain, then that's cool, too.

It was an incredibly anticlimactic moment. In the many dramatic hospital scenes I'd seen in movies and TV shows, being the young patient on her death bed after a rapid decline in bodily function is an eye-opening moment. Nothing mattered. My hair, skin, clothes, my car, my debt, my job... not even my 30 bracelets...nothing. I was in so much pain that death seemed a completely viable option even at 29 years old. Who knows what the next adventure is anyways?

November 2012

Photo by Thomas Turner. February 2012.

134

CHAPTER 10:

SHIFTING PERSPECTIVES

I was out in a borderline comatose state, sweating under the influence of morphine until the glare of the television woke me in what appeared to be the middle of the next night. Animal Planet's *Monster's Inside Me* was playing a premiere episode. As the television came into focus, I saw who I now know as Kay Howe and Graham McCumber.

Graham was dying, intubated, in a coma for months. His mother was by his side, feeding him natural herbs through his stomach tube. They had a diagnosis. It's a rare parasite, angiostrongylus cantonensis, A parasitic roundworm that attacks the central nervous system. Commonly known as Rat lungworm.

Wait, what?

How is it that the doctors here dealing with me had never heard of this until today, yet here I am watching a show highlighting the very rare sickness that is killing me on prime-time television? I didn't have enough energy to finish the show entirely. I tried desperately to stay awake, but my body was screaming, and I fell back to sleep in another puddle of my own morphine-induced sweat.

When my doctor came in to check on me, the next day, he had four med students in tow. They were changing my diaper, taking my temperature, checking my pic lines and saline levels, checking my lung biopsy puncture, giving me more sweat-inducing pain medication, scheduling more MRIs, and looking at me with concerned, unsure smiles. I was the first case of assumed angiostrongylus cantonensis anyone in that hospital had seen, so I was a bit of a freak show. The pain was too intense for me to really pay any of them much attention.

Physical therapy began immediately after my life was no longer in imminent danger. After a full day of observation, while my body was disposing of the parasites, slipping in and out of sweaty consciousness, I was taken to my first session. In the first physical therapy session, I was pushed into the room on a bed. I still didn't have the strength to hold on to anyone or anything enough to be lifted to a sitting position. I was lifted, growling through clenched teeth, to a padded table. The process involved three nurses because it was difficult to move me without touching me. My physical therapy task that day was to lift my feet from the surface any distance. I decided that that was what I would do. I flexed and lifted, a combination of growling whimpers while breathing heavily with effort but ultimately achieved nothing. My legs did not move. I tried multiple times with the same result. I tried until my physical therapist told me to stop. The task was changed to pointing my toes. I failed again, but there was a slight wiggle. I didn't feel it. I saw it.

When I was wheeled back to my room, the nurses changed my diaper and lifted me back into my assigned bed. They left the room, and I lost my composure completely, sobbing for more than twenty minutes before I could speak. I had failed at the most basic tasks needed to get back on my feet. At 29, for the first time in my life, I had absolutely and utterly failed at a simple physical task despite my best efforts. I was told by the infectious disease doctor directly, with no fluff, to not be optimistic about walking again. It didn't look like it would happen with the damage and parasitic infiltration he'd seen in the MRIs of my brain and body. I remained emotionless receiving that news. I knew in my heart he was wrong. I saw the wiggle.

I was stable and was told that I was moving from Intensive Care to the CLC2 inpatient area, where I had my own room. I was one of two females in the entire unit and the youngest by over 20 years. There I would stay indefinitely with a much older crew of Vietnam, Korean, and WWI veterans until I was ready to go home.

What a scary thought. I am 29 years old and planning to stay indefinitely in a nursing home in a wheelchair that I couldn't move, eating powdered fake eggs for breakfast with someone changing my diaper and brushing my hair for me. I couldn't bear that thought. I wanted a hard date to work towards with tangible goals to reach, so I didn't waste my time wishing I knew what to do to get back out into the world. I went on that show to purchase a wheelchair for my brother, not to live my entire life in one myself. The day after I was transferred to the CLC2, I met a different physical therapist and a different doctor, Dr. B. With them, I planned the path to regain my freedom.

I ambitiously decided that I wanted to leave on my own two feet by my 30th birthday, December 19th, 2012. In five weeks. I remembered in my early 20's being told by many older soldiers that my body would fall apart after 30, and I wouldn't be able to run anymore. However, as a young runner, I had read many *Runners' World* magazine articles highlighting really fast women winning races and titles who'd had incredible recoveries from physical destruction or hadn't even begun running until their 40s. I wanted to leave the hospital on my 30th birthday so that every day of my 30s, I would feel a little bit stronger. I would start at the bottom, so the only way to go is up. A simple perspective shift.

To reach this goal of giving myself the gift of freedom from my wheelchair on my 30th birthday, I needed to focus on the next step... Not the end goal of running or dancing again, not even the literal next full step. First, I needed to move my toes in a truly visible manner, lift my legs from that table, and learn how and where to put weight on my feet to achieve balance without falling. I needed to focus beyond the pain to feel the ground through burning pins and needles and sickening waves of ice and fire. Instead of Cross Fit or marathon training, I did drills in the mornings. Stretches that would help me eventually learn to bend my torso and my legs enough to put my socks on by myself and reach much more muscle failure and exhaustion. Some of these didn't even involve me taking off my blanket in bed. I chose to do physical therapy 2 times, sometimes 3 times a day.

My physical therapist and I agreed on a list of milestones that I must be able to hit before leaving the hospital to ensure to myself that I could live on my own two feet:

- One full squat
- Sit down without using my hands
- Put on my own socks and shoes
- Walk more than 200 feet without support
- Climb up and down a flight of stairs.
- Stand up from the ground without using my hands

Using the bathroom on my own was not included on that list because my body had to do that on its own. I set goals that would be a considerable challenge but were still manageable.

I made a basic promise to myself that I would make it to the cafeteria each and every morning for breakfast instead of staying in bed and waiting for the food to be delivered to me. This didn't mean I'd walk to breakfast; obviously, it meant that I would allow a nurse or my boyfriend or both to move me through kungfu worthy grunts to my wheelchair, then push me to the cafeteria before it closed at 10AM. This process could take almost an hour, sometimes more, because I was in so much pain. As excited as I was to train my body to recover, I honestly also had a healthy, undeniable fear of facing that much pain. It was the same hesitation I imagine someone would have before choosing to shoot themselves in the hand a second time in a row. Courage is not fearlessness. The fear stays on your shoulder, in a large portion of your mind, it narrows your focus and can freeze you in place at any point, if allowed, but it's what keeps you alive at the same time. Courage is doing the thing anyway, with every instinct telling you no. It's an incredibly close choice to stupidity.

There was no reprieve. The parasites were dead, but they had left my entire body on fire with waves of nauseating, misfiring nerves. The same skin sensitivity remained. My colon and bladder were not communicating with my brain correctly, and movement in those organs hurt as much as the razor-sharp air of any cool breeze. My nervous system wasn't allowing my body to regulate temperature. Every movement or temperature change felt like a mallet to my already shattered body. I understood why a wheelchair could be a tempting alternative to mewling in physical therapy to learn to "Franken-monster-walk."

I had a quiet conversation with myself to shift perspectives. I lived for the "torture" of a physically challenging race before any of this had happened. I had chosen to run the Copper Canyon 50-mile Ultra Marathon when I returned from Afghanistan. I was only trained for a 10K, but I still loved every grueling second of it. I finished 7th female and was hooked. In June, I had chosen the "Running with the Devil 50 miler" around Lake Meade, Nevada, with a Heat Index of close to 130 degrees Fahrenheit because it sounded like a "fun" challenge. Every true distance runner must be some form of masochist. So, if I wanted to sign up and pay money for the toughest races on the planet with a giant sh*t-eating grin, why not show up for them in my life in the same manner? I remember the middle of the night after I'd run the 50 miles in Copper Canyon, I needed to get out of bed to vomit because I had a heat injury, but I couldn't move my body and ended up crawling slowly. How epic had it been that I had chosen to travel and pay an entry fee to participate in a foot race up and down the canyon walls in order to feel that much pain in a tiny, scorpion-filled guest house in the middle of Urique, Mexico. Learning to walk again would have to be my next masochistic adventure for the immediate future.

Yes, it was going to hurt more than anything I'd ever done, but I could adjust to deal with pain. That's something with which I've had decent experience compartmentalizing. I just needed to dedicate the time to train and retrain my body to function and learn to accept this different pain payment plan throughout the process. I was given an opportunity to challenge my resolve like never before, and I was determined to take advantage of it.

That said, I was not immune to the spirit-crushing, distracting, enraging, depressing effect of extreme lifestyle change due to paralysis and immense amounts of nerve pain. I just recognized it as something I needed to handle face-on and immediately. I didn't want to skip it or wait for it to stop hurting in order to smile and feel thankful for breathing because this, too, was a moment of my life that I would never have the chance to live again. My time spent residing in the nursing home was time spent living. My self-selected challenges changed from carrying myself up and down incredibly savage canyon walls on my own two feet to lifting those same two feet off a bed and learning to use them again through a different style of mind-numbing pain. My signature block since 2007 on all emails had been a saying by Paulo Coehlo that I loved, "The danger of an adventure is worth 1,000 days of ease and comfort." Well, I'd gone on my adventure, and I guess the ease took its leave. This was what I had chosen. I had put that slug in my mouth, and now it was my adventure to experience.

To keep a smile on my face, I needed to be in the present. Not in the past. Not in the future. In order to do that, I needed to learn to separate each moment as a different experience. Back to the "each moment you live is the last time you live that moment." I couldn't afford to label an entire day as bad in my mind. That could lead to a dangerous depression. There were simply some unfortunate moments that usually could be spun into something positive.

There was a lush, fragrant rose garden behind the hospital that I was enchanted with visiting every chance possible to take the deepest of breaths. It never failed. After the first full breath, if it took that long, I was smiling gently at the instant stimulation of sensual therapy. What a gift to have such a vibrant sanctuary right on the hospital grounds. At first, I could barely withstand the wheelchair ride. It was bone-crushing pain to hit bumps on the sidewalk. Still, nobody wants to continue pushing someone in a wheelchair when they are vocally expressing extreme pain from the exact help you are giving. I'd be left exhausted by the time I reached the flower. Not only from the pain itself but from clenching my jaw and attempting to passively observe the pain with less and less audible noise each trip. I'd notice my eyes sliding in and out of focus on my knees, the throbbing of my temples while the cold fire burned my spine, torso, and limbs relentlessly. I held the armrests of the wheelchair with white knuckles. The pain was apparent in every cell of my body, just not my voice, and that's how I convinced the reluctant ones with healthy bodies to allow me to make the healing trips. Those were the 2-mile climbs to Hurricane Point I'd run in the Big Sur Marathon just a few years prior. Those rides to the garden were the "opportunities disguised as work." The payment was the view, with a side of olfactory stimulation, and in the case of the race, an angelic pianist playing for your ascent as the ocean breeze tickles the back of your neck. The reality is, even on the last day in the hospital, my pain had not lessened, just as the Climb to Hurricane Point didn't change its difficulty. I began to get slightly better at processing this new style of pain when I actively paid attention. It felt the same as when I trained to run that winding mountain hard without dropping my speed or form.

Everything I wanted to change about me was changeable, but it would take time dedicated to the task to improve. In the past, I'd spent afternoons doing interval hill training, driving my knees up against the heavy pressure of lactic acid, my chest out, my chin up. Now, I was doing repetitions of keeping my jaw slack and unfurrowing my brow during extreme pain to normalize keeping my face presentable and pleasant while the internal electrical shocks continued.

When I went to the rose garden, I passed a grassy hill overlooking a duck pond. I dreamed of walking up that hill every single time I saw it, knowing I would do it like I'd looked at mountain ridges and imagined running them in the past. When I'd finally gotten strong enough to push a walker for short distances, I began to practice my new version of "hill training." Sometimes I'd make it a step or two before needing to stop, other times, I could make three or four. Each attempt was grueling, but the progress was the pianist playing at the climax. Nirvana.

On the morning of my 30th birthday, I left my wheelchair behind and hobbled out of the hospital. I was leaning on my walker with both hands. My hips were still not rotating correctly, so I had a very round look to my steps as if I needed to walk around my hips. On my way out, I saw the doctor who saved my life. The man in the emergency room who decided I deserved to be an inpatient and obviously wasn't a drug addict. I took a picture with him and continued on to the hill.

Face to face with my biggest goal for my recovery in the hospital, I was determined to walk up that hill without my walker. I left my walker at the bottom and began to awkwardly wobble my way up. I wanted to have a pancake birthday breakfast overlooking the duck pond to celebrate the beginning of my 30s as a free woman. What a victory! I was in tears when I hit the top, an all-encompassing elation. I had done it. I had given myself the gift of reaching the first checkpoint in this ultra-grueling stage race of recovery: Freedom from the nursing home without my wheel-chair in tow.

CHAPTER 11:

THE RECOVERY CONTINUES

I was given an opportunity few receive. I watched my 5'4 frame wither away to less than 100lbs, and my mental capacities dwindle to nearly nothing before being rebuilt. I rose from my death bed to live again. As a passive observer, I saw my reflexes disappear with my equilibrium and my colon and bladder malfunction from poor communication with my brain, which was drowning in meningitis. Diapers at 29. I know the fury of having clear thoughts without the language nor the physical capacity to communicate them efficiently. I was shown that, beyond any doubt, I am organic. My heart will stop beating. One day my body will stop functioning completely, and I will move on to the next adventure.

I have been given a close glimpse of the destination: Death. I heard a newly admitted veteran lose his life in the room next to me and listened to the nurses trying to revive him for almost an hour without success. I looked into the eyes of a doctor who showed his clear concern that I was dying and another who didn't believe I would ever take another step of my own volition.

Yet, I walked out of that hospital to live. Bent over, shoulders high, chest clenched, neck and traps flexed tightly in a defensive position as I leaned heavily on my walker, I walked. I smiled as I felt my father's pride warm my back in the form of the Arizona December sun's gentle morning caress.

When I left the Phoenix VA Healthcare System, I headed to Pennsylvania. The original plan had been to help my stepmother after my father's suicide, but now I was the one who needed help. The table had turned.

Reaching the first checkpoint in no way meant that the recovery was over, not even close. But I felt like it could be if I pushed the way I naturally pushed during the harder sections of a run. I knew I would run again. I never had limits before, and it was a hard thing to begin to understand.

My brain still thought I was able-bodied like it still thought I was in war every time I heard an explosion, although it was more than clear that I wasn't. I found myself looking at mountains and planning approaches again. Thinking about races, dancing, traveling, and camping in remote places where I needed to rely on my own power to live.

I was beginning to learn about my very-obvious limits. Obvious to everyone but my own brain. They changed daily. It was as if there was an invisible line that I could overstep in my daily tasks and attempts to get stronger that would make the night nearly unbearable in terms of pain payment plan and muscle spasms. The tricky part was that the line seemed to be mobile. Sometimes it only took a small amount of movement to be bed laden for the entire evening, other days much more. Still, I always felt a distinct change in my body when I had crossed it.

As a follow up, I went to see a neurologist at the Lebanon VA Hospital. When I was called back to her office, she stopped me at the door, holding my dictionary thick medical file in her hands.

Clearly disbelieving, she stuttered, "You're Maldonado? I read your file. How? How are you...How are you standing in front of me?" She almost touched me, but pulled back her hands at the last second, as if she feared she might get burned. "I read your file. You shouldn't...You...Wow." She continued to look me up and down. "You should be dead. I mean, I read your file, but you look healthy." She gestured to my cane and said, "And you're walking! I read your file! You had a glucose level of 27. You should be dead. Wow. You are a miracle. Come into my office."

She went on to explain to me that the only way she can imagine that I survived a case of rat lungworm disease as serious as mine was a direct result of my addiction to activities that required extreme endurance: the type that literally begin to starve your brain as it runs out of glucose in your system. The 50-mile race in the deepest canyon in North America, the 4 days of not eating while hiking 18-30 miles daily followed by another 3 weeks of less than 700 calories a day while covering equally challenging terrain, the 50-mile race around Lake Meade, Nevada in June sporting temperatures upwards of 115 degrees Fahrenheit. I had taken my brain on enough crazy endurance adventures that she had become familiar with the "training" and instead of slipping into a coma when the parasites were eating me alive, She held me on the cusp like a gristled combat veteran muttering, "Not my first rodeo." The neurologist explained that feeding my desire to train for and race extreme distances on extreme terrain in extreme temperatures had ultimately saved my life. I'd essentially trained myself to beat these parasites my entire life. What a concept to consider.

Had I ignored my desire to do things my own way, I very well could be dead or still in a wheelchair asking for help to brush my own hair, "T-t-t-top?"

At my stepmother's house I was waking up in my father's room, with his energy everywhere. I felt desperate to be kind to the world and to myself. Yet my body screamed at me every second of the day in chorus with my boyfriend "caretaker," who staunchly disagreed with my decision to forgive everyone as quickly as possible to release my own self-poisoning rage and numbing sadness. It was my way to attempt to remain in the present moment, but to him it was weakness.

The way I'd chosen to attempt to accept my father's suicide was by seeing it as his choice. If I was going to work hard to accept that desperate and painful decision, then I felt it would be hypocritical to not accept the decisions of others as their own, most of which have nothing to do with me. I mean, how would I feel if people got mad at me for making a choice I felt I needed to make to heal myself? The society in which we are expected to "live" is one where people would rather commit suicide than live, so I extracted myself nearly completely.

My father and I had both left society, albeit in different ways. I gave away or sold everything I owned... He left it all behind. This included the things he stored for me when he decided that I wasn't serious about wanting to sell it. He left everything he knew for a new start. I drove alone with a voice recorder and two dogs to a cabin 10 miles outside of Haines, Alaska, with no cell reception, and screamed and sobbed into the sky for solid chunks of time, without contacting anyone for days at a time. I'd thought of running away as a kid often. As an adult, I finally had the freedom to do it. So, I did. We both had abandoned everything and everyone to start over. How could I judge him for that?

There were nights where the woman I'd called Mom since I was 7 would show up sobbing uncontrollably, and I sobbed with her. We held each other, sharing tears of loss. Confusion. My father chose to leave, her partner chose to leave. I'd looked at his frail, hollow, waxy corps, as she had. I had held his ashes hot to my chest. She had done the same. What a challenging thing to accept! How did he choose to leave right before I got paralyzed, when he was the only person in the family that had any medical knowledge? The only one who had chosen me. But this, too, was his decision to make.

I watched her go through feelings and reactions that I didn't experience through our grief for the passing of the same man. Her anger was fierce. My only response to it was that I had no idea how it felt to lose the person with whom I'd shared the last 22 years of my life. How could I judge or even begin to have an opinion on how she acted? My boyfriend angrily disagreed with the acceptance for which I strived and felt that I should be angry as well. This caused problems (that already existed in a big way) between us. She spent a few days celebrating his death in front of me, a direct result of extreme anger and sadness. There's no offense to take when you can clearly see that it is coming from a place of intense pain that you know you cannot understand. Some nights were full of drinking and dancing, others spent with another man. Every step of the way, 1 watched an absolutely broken woman fight to accept the hardest news I could imagine receiving, and I was being yelled at by my loving boyfriend for not being angry at her attempts to survive her grieving process. Grief is messy. It looks and feels ugly. There is simply no rule for anyone about how to do it. It hits at the most random, sudden times and hard. I found myself grieving for both my father and myself because I wasn't given the space to handle mine the way I needed to. I didn't have the physical capacity to leave and take the time for myself the way I wanted to.

Every day, I followed a chair yoga DVD that Sue Arnold, my life-long mentor and 9th-grade science teacher from Milton Hershey School, had sent me for my birthday/hospital discharge to build up the flexibility to do real yoga and hopefully walk without an extreme limp. I did chair yoga, slowly changing poses with the DVD paused until I could catch up with the teacher. After a couple of weeks, I gained some strength with chair yoga, and I began to do yoga with a Rodney Yee DVD that Rosa had sent for the same celebration. Changing poses on the floor took much more time, sometimes upwards of 5 minutes, to move my healing body into a position. The normally 40-minute session could easily take almost 2 hours, but I never stopped the DVD without finishing the entire routine. I was taking short, slow, painful, but blissful walks around the block with either my cane or walker, depending on the day. It was time to do more.

The first time I went to Zumba, I made it through 1 wobbly song. I did not fall, although I came close several times. Unlike life, when you have a million things going on at once, a moment on the dance floor has one. Just one. The music. Nothing bothers you; nothing can bother you. It takes 100% of your attention. Your troubles are flung from your person in a head whip, a hand flip, a kung fu dip. Charged, they spring from your extended fingers, carrying your energy, your current. Tossed from your hair as your vibrant curls slice through the air. Gone.

In those moments of that song, I hadn't just been in the hospital. I wasn't a combat-wounded veteran with PTSD, mourning my father's suicide and the death of my own invincibility complex. I had a clean slate. I became the music. My body; the instrument that makes the song complete. The lack of equilibrium I suffered added an element of adventure and danger to the entire experience that really got me high. That night I couldn't stop smiling, despite the intense pain payment plan and spasms I'd earned by dancing. It was worth it for the feeling I had dancing like that again. Nirvana is a paw in motion. That moment is the Zen of dancing in the rain, of movement through life, the cleansing of your soul and spirit.

My boyfriend was the one that did yoga with me. He helped me, spending hours on the task at a time. At the same time, he treated me as if my paralysis wasn't something that happened to me so much as something I was choosing to do to him, an incredibly difficult dichotomy. An absolute Jeckel and Hyde. He reminded me verbally that I was incapable of doing any of it without him whenever he felt I wasn't thanking him enough. I found myself switching between gratefulness, sadness, grief, helplessness, and shame for staying under his thumb. I showered him with public positivity, skipping over every low and focusing on all the positive aspects of our relationship. It was like searching for the silver lining of the mushroom cloud, daily, relentlessly. Still, it was feeling less and less real as time went on. As such, insecurities grew. My thoughts, words, and actions were not aligning.

I was ashamed of every argument we had, especially when I had chosen to participate. Every time somebody challenged his behavior to me after spending time with us, I'd instantly jump to defend him like a starving stray dog, snarling, hackles raised, ready to protect its rotten meal to the death. Being with him had been my decision, and at that time, I felt that the success of that relationship was a direct reflection of me and my choices. I felt I couldn't leave without admitting to the world that the man I had been praising as a savior and saint to everyone often chose to be incredibly cruel to me. I stayed way longer than I felt any self-respecting woman would or should because deep down, in my darkest of thoughts, I felt that I deserved it. My thoughts, words, and actions were not aligned. I found myself newly concerned about judgments from others because I was judging myself, the exact thing I had spent years feeling like I'd mastered.

He called me a hypocrite. Deep down, it touched an insecurity I was harboring since I recognized that I wasn't following the lessons I had thought I had mastered. Sometimes I was failing miserably in a pile of snot and tears. The journey of correcting one's actions and thoughts, of truly living authentically through life's challenges while being kind to yourself as your own best friend, is not a basic cut-and-dry inspirational post on social media like you might think. It's a brutal journey of which there is no map distinctly tailored to your experience. It's a constant check-in process that requires delving into the places you don't like to visit, and just like any muscle, your brain gets tired and sometimes injured. I don't know how many times I sprained my ankle running or playing basketball, but if you want to continue to play, you nurse that sh*t back. Same for life and the brain. It includes learning to forgive yourself quickly for the moments that break you and everything else in between.

He'd told me nobody would want me if I left him, and deep down, that touched another insecurity. My father had just committed suicide, and my mother had literally abandoned me in a house as a baby and not shown up to the court to keep me. Now, my bladder and colon were not functioning, and I was still using a cane or walker to walk outside the house. I was having bathroom accidents often and was in incredible pain. I was taking obscene amounts of Gabapentin, an antidepressant that has an off-script usage for nerve pain, made by Pfizer, a company that has been taken to court for the connection between their medication and suicidal thoughts. The reality, though, is that I didn't want to need to be saved by anyone. A large part of me felt I was paying for my part in the suffering of this world. I had played a militant role in little girls losing their fathers, and now I knew what pain I had bestowed. It was inexcusable cruelty for which I felt I needed to pay, and knowing that self-sacrifice is the Army way, it was something I continued to sign up for.

Sometimes I would feel moments of dissatisfaction with my progress. I'd forget to be my own best friend in moments full of tears and hopelessness, pain, desperation, and shame. During one of those nights, I decided I needed to make a change. I was sitting in the living room having a snack, and my arm spasmed so hard that I stabbed myself in the head with a fork. I had a moment of amused wonder. I had spent years mastering body movements and isolations, but now my body moved by itself in big, weird ways. I sat thinking about the *Monsters Inside Me* episode that I had seen in the hospital and how I hadn't finished it. I wanted to see how it ended and maybe contact the woman, her son, or both.

I did a quick search online and found the episode, watched it, and immediately understood why it had been better for me to have fallen asleep in the hospital than see the ending. I had no idea that Graham had so many lasting difficulties with movement and function, and I had attacked my sickness with an innocent determination ignorant of the other struggling survivors of the same illness. I found Kay Howe on Facebook and sent her a message. We began a friendship through our shared experiences with rat lungworm. Since there was no real solid source for public education, we began to share notes on what we were doing in our own recoveries. I explained to Kay that I needed to go somewhere to recover that wasn't my father and stepmother's home. She immediately recommended Moab, Utah. It took a solid 5 seconds for me to decide to move there. I had already visited two times and had been impressed by the towering red sandstone, snow-capped La Sal mountains, dinosaur footprints, and fossils left behind. Those rocks were obviously there before our species was born and will

161

continue long after we've decomposed and become one with Mother Earth once again. It is a place that takes you out of yourself and reminds you that you indeed do not matter.

It was time to move away from the bustle of central Pennsylvania and head to Moab. My loving boyfriend had thrown a chair while screaming, berating me over whatever I had done to offend him that specific morning, and had broken my stepmother's door. That was beyond the last straw for her. She was grieving, and we were occupying her space. No longer a blessing but an obstacle, and she needed to begin to regain her peace again. One day, she left a note on the refrigerator, saying that we needed to leave. My things were locked out of the house, the locks were changed, and my father's ashes were left for me in a $30 blue and white hand-held cooler. She blocked me on social media, sold the house to her cousin, and moved to Hawaii with the $50,000 life insurance money from my father's death to begin a business with her daughter. My older sister, Amara shattered my heart at the same time, lashing out hatefully, attacking just about every one of my insecurities in one message when I finally confided in a family member that I was having violent, suicidal dreams. I felt uncharacteristically angry through my weaning from Gabapentin mixed with my father's suicide. I admitted that I feared my violent dreams.

She wrote: "Will you dream of bashing my head into an oncoming train? Will you stab Serena in her sleep the next time she expresses something through her art? Will you wish your brothers in a car crash with their wives because they simply have lives that don't include you? You scream from the mountain top: Look at MEEEEEE I'm wounded!!! I'm a wounded vet who ran an ultramarathon soon after my second war! I served my country, and my country doesn't serve me! (Yet you took EVERY bonus EVERYTIME YOU reenlisted). You enlisted because YOU wanted a free ride. You enlisted because you got PAID. You signed up, not for your country but for you. You got sick because YOU wanted to scream from the rooftop, hey look at me, look at me I'm on a TV show. You ate the f*ckin slug and you got sick. Your father killed himself, did YOU pay enough attention to him? How many times did he visit you? Did he go to AK? Did he go to HI? He put you in a boarding school and let someone else raise you," before blocking me on every social media platform for years.

I immediately felt like I couldn't contact any other family because these were the ones with whom I had been closest, the ones I trusted with the truth, and they had all turned their backs on me as a result. My sister had acted as a self-appointed gate keeper of the family on my mother's side, and depending on her mood, the rest of us were either in the circle of trust or out. If you were out, it was a few degrees more than basic banishment. I didn't understand her constant efforts to control other people's social decisions, but since she had always organized to be the one that brought me to see my aunts and my cousins, I felt that her hate could be contagious. I felt that they, too, might reject me, so I stayed away. I convinced myself that it must be me. I was no longer the invincible, golden, scholar-athlete warrior with the crazy high tolerance for pain. I was in diapers with invisible injuries, and I needed to get over it and stop b*tching because I looked fine. The empathy gap was a canyon. Reports came to me from multiple other family members that it was forbidden to even mention my name in her house. I was Uncle Bruno. It took me years to even have the courage to look at the situation to begin understanding what had happened. Even now, the battle I'm having with including the message from my big sister is unfair to myself, as I promised I wouldn't censor myself in my healing, my writing, and therefore that should naturally extend to my book.

I would include all things a stranger had done without hesitation, but the fact that this person is somebody I know intimately makes me want to hide it. Still, this message was integral to my story and eventual healing. This message turned my already scary rage into something all-consuming that made suicide more than an idea to explore. It was a growing self-loathing. These people didn't understand my heart. They hadn't even glanced at my shoes to consider walking in them. They would go out of their way to hurt me using words they didn't even begin to understand, on the topics most volatile in my world, based only on their projected observations and personal turmoil. Intentionally trying to hurt me. I couldn't figure out what emotion it was, but it wasn't love. I couldn't dig up the lessons I had sworn I understood in Alaska at 27 when I began my healing journey: "hurt people hurt people," and "all judgments stem from one's own insecurities." I dug them up, but they were just words. They didn't resonate like they once had. Nobody had told me that I would have to learn these lessons, then learn them again. Nobody had explained that the journey to self-acceptance and authenticity was not a once and done process. I couldn't feel sorry for her struggles in her journey because my own were drowning me. I'd completely lost my way in my mastery of self.

At that time, I felt abandoned by everyone to whom I turned, leaving me with only my "loving boyfriend," whom I seemed to accidentally enrage constantly. It was the lowest time in my life. So low that I loaded the same 9 mm that my father used and held it in my own mouth alone in the conversion van I had bought and turned into a home to live my dream. The cold metal clicked against my teeth as I gripped it, shaking. Hating. Enraged. Desperate. Lost. Nobody interrupted that moment, I just didn't feel the absolute desire to pull the trigger from deep down in my soul, so I didn't. Everything in my thoughts was hate towards others, and circumstance, yet suicide felt like self-sacrifice to spite them. The hatred wasn't inward. There was a calm light deep in the depths of darkness that stayed burning, the mountain that stays rooted as the storm rages and erodes her face. When I finally noticed it, I allowed it to guide me from my rabbit hole. There had to be another way to live.

I felt a rage that I had never experienced before. A rage that I hadn't known was possible. It mostly manifested in my sleep. I dreamt of doing the most horrid things. I killed them often. Murdering and

166

torturing them in explicit ways that mimicked my tortured mind and broken heart. I allowed their words to carve out holes in my soul that had been reserved for love and acceptance. Hate crept in without hesitation, attacking me in my dreams in antagonistic harmony with my manipulated memories of combat. I was worried because it felt so cyclic. Every morning after, I felt a subtle concern for my mental health and smoldering rage that I then tucked down because with whom can one talk about things like that?

What Hell that was, and all the time I was dancing. I went to Zumba every day, filling hours of my days with music and laughter. I used all my tools to compartmentalize the pain and to move my body to the rhythm of life because that was the deck of cards I had been given. Or better stated, I was the dealer, and that was the deck of cards I'd dealt myself. After arriving in Pennsylvania, working on yoga daily, walking, and attending Zumba, I built up enough endurance to begin teaching a full class of Zumba. I had already become a Zumba instructor just after leaving the army in 2010, and I felt like if I made a commitment to teaching, I would never shirk my responsibility of dancing my heart out, clearing my mind, finding my center, and ultimately making headway in my recovery. So, in March of 2013, just four months after Franken-walked out of the hospital, I began to teach Zumba 2 times a week.

The music has a way of numbing even the most severe pains, and I was already learning shortcuts in my movements to make up for my balance, strength, and endurance deficiencies. My excitement for the blessing of being able to dance and my gratitude for movement was contagious. I lived for those classes, celebrating every breath by digging beyond lactic acid from the very first step. My legs were leaden, fire and ice were unleashed in my limbs each time I shifted weight. It hurt badly, and my screams in class were of the kind you hear from a feral distance runner who has just burned her way up a mountain and can't help but release at the top. The kind of euphoric agony that echoes through mountains and into valleys. Sheer pain and wild elation. The scream that lifts you off the ground and makes the arteries in your neck pop out while your cheeks turn a crimson hue.

Then the songs would end, we would do our cooldown routine, and as we came down from our dance highs, my body began to howl with frayed nerve endings and throbbing feet. The energy I'd exerted made walking a much larger task. I found myself then hobbling slowly off the dance floor, an entire basketball court, trying not to ask anyone for help,

168

focused only on the spot just in front of me, lest I fall. When I reached the car, it would take nearly a full 30 seconds to take a seat. The movement was always accompanied by a grunt worthy of a combat kung-fu gesture. I would always park close to the door because I had my handicapped tag. The rest of the night, I'd spend mewling and spasming with a giant strained smile.

By the time I moved on to Moab, I had connected with quite a great dance community in Central Pennsylvania. They supported me, lifting me up in a way that perhaps they never even recognized. To them, it was a Zumba class with an exuberantly happy, goofy teacher. To me, it was the rope to which I clung with both hands and both legs to not only survive but to find moments of Zen through the storm. Their excitement for my classes was what I used to stifle the pain and work harder. The runner sometimes can draw additional energy from a supporter's energy alongside the trail. Our shared sweaty moments of silliness and unbridled laughter masked the fact that sometimes I lost my balance, sometimes my bladder malfunctioned a little or a lot, and every class was incredibly painful and exhausting.

CHAPTER 12:

MOAB SALSA BACHATA FESTIVAL

I know how it feels to celebrate a shower alone as a milestone, and I fully recognize the gift of simply being able to walk without help. When I arrived in Moab, I found myself sitting in the shade, watching people walk in the streets and noticing that many of them were fit and had strong legs. I had changed my dogma that I would run again soon. Well, I began to understand that my stubbornness and pain tolerance wasn't going to be enough to immediately regain some of my activities without serious sacrifice. I began to focus on other activities to keep my mind busy while challenging my body and recovering. I set up my slackline, went climbing, hiking, and mountain biking (which turned into an entire new obsession), and danced, of course.

In my first week in Moab, I dropped by the Moab Arts and Recreation Center, and I checked to see if there were already salsa or bachata dance lessons or socials happening. There were not, but the building was equipped with a large, beautiful dance room lined with mirrors. I was sold. I decided that I needed to create a dance scene in Moab, Utah, so that I could continue my healing and have a commitment to move daily.

My first salsa class was on the front page of the Moab Sun newspaper. I steadily promoted, walking from business to business, meeting people, sharing a bit of my story, and putting up flyers. Dropping tiny seeds of inspiration along the way. I began teaching beginner salsa, but soon I had students in different levels taking different classes: beginner, intermediate, specialized body movement classes, performance classes, ladies styling, combinations, and shines. After a while, I was teaching bachata, Zumba, and Masala Bhangra, an Indian-inspired endurance dance workout as well.

However, my soul was truly filled in the after-school program I was offering for the Charter public elementary schools on alternating days. I was teaching children ages 7-11. I asked to volunteer in the first trimester because their funds were already used.

To my surprise, they picked me up as an employee the next trimester. I used my story of paralysis as an inspirational teaching tool because it was still apparent that I was in pain. Sometimes I lost my balance. One time I even lost my bowels, though not in front of the kids' class. It was an adult class from which I needed to excuse myself. I became accustomed to having an extra change of pants and underwear with me staged just outside the studio bathroom, so if I had an accident, I could quickly excuse myself and handle my affair without too much fanfare.

Eventually, I organized some flash mobs and directed a community-funded dance team, Salsa Picante. In an effort to bring children and families together over dance and recycling, we made our dresses from donated T-shirts the local thrift shop, Wabi Sabi, provided. My goal was to show them that there are more paths than the well-trodden one to take, and if they wanted it, they could make it happen.

I created for them a practice studio with donated mirrors stacked against walls. We created our dresses from donations, but the biggest way I thought to prove to them that they can make anything happen if they just think outside of the box and take the time to develop a dream was by creating a salsa band out of willing musicians that lived in Moab. Kokopelli

Tropical was born because to build the style dance scene that I wanted, I needed to inspire people to learn salsa for more than a class or two. To do this, I needed an event monthly where they'd be excited to go dance. I knew the songs like a dancer, inside and out. The musicians knew the instruments. I knew the clave and the cues, down to the solos and accents, and so could cue them all more effectively than our bass player. I had the most interesting combination of instruments for some really beautiful renditions of classic songs. My horn section was a flute and a harmonica. My rhythm section was congas, bongo, maracas, clave, guitar, base, and even a mandolin. We played a cover of Tito Puente's Ran Kan Kan, a song completely about the sound that is made by the timbales, without timbales. The kids loved it. Adults are just big kids with more insecurities. They loved it, too.

Every second I spent teaching dance with these children was perfectly exquisite. I watched shy, timid girls become empowered, kind, confident flowers on stage and in life. They performed the opening act in the Moab Valley Multicultural Center's first annual *Dancing with the Moab Stars* competition, and they were fabulous. For that competition, I had been paired up with the Mayor of Moab, Dave Sakrison. We performed a Bacha-Tango, a fusion of Bachata and Tango.

We won, wearing recycled outfits with fancy edging that my soul sister, "Freaka," had constructed from emergency blankets and other salvaged items.

The kids and I shared some truly teachable moments together. One time, we were gathering in the cafeteria with the entire after-school crowd of kids, seated at different tables. There had been a celebration that day, maybe a student's birthday, and there were a handful of balloons being bounced around. While I was in the middle of addressing my group, one of the students directly behind me stepped on and popped a balloon. The entire cafeteria fell silent for a moment then erupted into wails of laughter when they all realized what had actually happened. Miss Rita screamed and dove under the table really fast! What a crazy lady!

I stood up, already laughing because I had the realization after I was already on the ground that the situation wasn't what my brain said it was. Elementary school after-school program not combat. I saw an opportunity to teach compassion without guilt or shame for having enjoyed a funny moment because, from their standpoint and mine, it was giggle-worthy. After the laughter died down, my group and I had a chat. I told them the truth about why I dove. There was a little nervous laughter but mostly pensive eyes.

175

Every class, we went over 4 vocabulary words before anything.

- Choreography
- Musicality
- Empowerment
- Degradation

I realized in having these classes that I could create the curriculum based on what I wanted to share outside of the box. It was important to me that they learn the definitions of empowerment and degradation. The beginning of correcting any habit is recognition. I asked them for examples of each daily. The goal was to instill that there are always other ways to respond than the ways they may have been taught. I wanted them to understand that there is an alternative to degrading someone or themselves and that they could choose to be intentionally kind. Each time they worked a drill, I had them tell me which variation to the steps they had made, focusing only on their own performance and accepting complete responsibility for their own actions. There can be many life lessons taught in a dance class beyond basic addition, fractions, and multiplication. Only when one understands the actual mistake can one truly fix it... but since there are no mistakes in dance, just variations, it makes it all O.K.

I taught kids during the day, adults at night, and drove to Salt Lake City to dance on the weekends. I paid heavily for my excitement to move with pain, still recovering from rat lungworm with wonky balance and skin sensitivity. One of the first times I'd gone to Chocolat, a club on Main Street, I asked a gentle giant named Nexar to dance. He had fantastic energy and a quick smile. One of the dancers that always looked like he was having fun. Crazy curls and big dimples. We danced a smooth mambo. I focused on my balance, keeping my weight on the balls of my feet and my legs moving while absolutely beaming with love for a non-vocal, playful conversation on clave.

He prepared me for what felt like a triple spin, and when he went to lead the turn, I fell flat on my face. Dropped like a fly in the middle of the club, in front of everyone. In less than a bar of music, I'd jumped back up, adrenaline and desperation fueling me through the pain, and grabbed him, whispering softly, nearly begging, "Please keep dancing with me. I'm ok. Please, just please finish the song with me. Please." His face mirrored something of horror and confusion. Shock, Humiliation, and disbelief flashed in his eyes, but he picked me up on the next clave, and we finished that

177

dance. To him, it was a dance he thought he'd messed up; to me, it was so much more. I'd fallen, sober, on the floor in the middle of the club after being told I wouldn't walk again. I stood back up from the ground quickly (the hardest task in physical therapy), and I hadn't turned away from finishing the dance. I cried that night. Rivers of gratitude for movement and for the kindness of that man who had no clue what he had done for me.

As I got stronger with my own balance, I began to do solo spins again. One night I was social dancing with a student of mine at Woody's Tavern in Moab, and I released her to shine and prepped for a double spin. Somehow I found myself falling, so I guided myself towards the stage where my drink was sitting. I managed to use my momentum to turn around and sit down, scoop up my white Russian as I crossed my legs, take a sip, and jump back up for the next cross-body lead, laughing hysterically. If you stumble, do it in style. Make it part of the dance. Every "mistake" is just another creative variation. There are no mistakes in dance. Just variations.

The Moab Salsa Bachata Festival came about when I learned that the Moab Travel Council was offering grant money to promote events that brought tourists in the off-season winter months. I had never filled out a grant before. Melissa Schmaedick, director of the Moab Music Festival and a mother of one of my dance students, offered to help and gave me the format of the budget spreadsheet and several helpful tools to assist in organizing the paperwork. I spent weeks at the beautiful library, plugging away at spreadsheets to apply for the grant and got it! Immediately, I needed to set to work to organize this dance festival that would be over Veteran's Day Weekend and free for veterans.

I had been awarded funds to promote the festival in person at the Phoenix, Grand Canyon, and Las Vegas Salsa Festivals and the Denver Salsa Bachata Congress. I asked one of my friends, Jorge Elizondo, the creator of bachata fusion and Dallas Bachata Festival organizer, to help with the project. He agreed to work with me. I went and paid attention to what they were doing while taking the opportunity to train. I learned what I did and didn't want to do with mine. I realized that, with this festival, I got to create a party that is exactly how I wanted it to be. I focused on creating the positive energy that I wanted to experience and share.

I had a platform to bring people of all shapes and sizes into the same beautiful and humbling scenery. There are towering red rocks and deep wild canyons carved with water, sand, and wind that follow the mighty Colorado River right through the center of town. There are still dinosaur footprints and giant bones peeking out of the rock at viewpoints. It is old, and obviously so. Moab reminds you that if you fall off a cliff, nothing will change, and so it makes you more of a human being.

I had some of the best dancers in the world mingling with some of the best climbers and mountain bikers on and off the dance floor. I took them all out of their comfort zones, and friends were made where there could easily have been a divide. Everyone was an absolute beginner at something they did that weekend.

I got rid of the style of Master of Ceremonies most festivals were using. I took out the degrading jokes that made beginner dancers feel uncomfortable or were unsuitable for children. Instead, I invited Sekou McMiller, a beautifully inspirational spirit from Alvin Ailey Dance Co in New York and took out the skits between the professional performances. I replaced them with stories of dancers who had had devastating injuries or illnesses and used dance to make a major comeback in a display I called "Gratitude for Movement." We performed a soul-stirring tribute to veterans as the night's last show before the social dancing began on Veteran's Day. On the last day of the festival, there were options for dance adventures.

Some dancers went up to Cable Arch and danced on top of the giant rock eroded by wind and rain before repelling down. Some went on a guided RazR tour and danced on the red rocks, while others went on a hike in Arches National Park. It was a fantastic weekend.

In 2015 I was promoting my festival at the Denver Salsa Bachata Congress. A woman approached me as I left the stage. She showed me her guesthouse information and said that she wanted me to come to Vieques, Puerto Rico and see if it sounded viable to throw a festival there with the same "Gratitude for Movement" theme. I thought about my calendar and told her I would keep it in mind, but 2015 and 2016 were already booked.

In August 2016, after a particularly ugly fight with my loving boyfriend, he went to work, and I drank to forget and earn my do-over for the day. It was still the morning. I noticed I had a text message from my friend Mimy, asking how I was doing. I told her the truth, exactly how I was doing, and what had just happened. She didn't ask anything more; she told me she was sending someone. Three friends arrived less than 15 minutes after I sent the text to help me get my things out of the house and whisk me away. Lara Gale, Aaron Lindberg, and Natalie Dayy.

Lara said flatly, "You're leaving, right?" as more of a statement than a question, and took my drunken, swollen, sad, disheveled look as a confirmation. When they had arrived, I was more than tipsy, so they told me not to worry about anything, to point at things that were mine, and they would load them in the car and take them wherever I directed. That is how I regained my freedom. It was not my own courage or taking my fear with me and finally leaving, but a drunken confession of a secret I had kept deep and dark to a friend who immediately stepped in and helped. Thank you, Lara, Mimy, Aaron and Natalie.

I continued organizing the last 3 months before the Moab Salsa Bachata Festival while sleeping in a damp 1980s camper behind my friend's house. After the Moab Salsa Bachata Festival ended in November of 2016, the hotel I was using let me know that they wouldn't be able to host the event in 2017, the beautiful Moab Arts & Recreation Center space that I had been using had decided to double the price of my rental for 2017, and the space I was using to train my young community-funded team was not going to be available any longer. My now ex was threatening to burn my things since he'd lost control. I felt it necessary to leave Moab rather quickly once the visiting instructors moved on to their next locations.

Life happens. We are all organic. I learned precisely how organic I was in the hospital, consciously watching myself lose all my faculties one by one until I was under 100 lbs and gray. Dying. A person's thoughts, words, and actions must align for peace to creep into one's soul. I knew the words, but I truly understand now that my heart will cease to beat. I will absolutely die, as will every person I know, and since that is true, when my soul tells me that I must do something good, I have no choice but to listen. I had thought of leaving Moab and my ex for years. I had thought of going to Puerto Rico, back to my island, back to be one with the Earth, since I'd had a dream about it at 4 years old. The dream stayed with me my entire life: an image of a tiny wooden house with a tin roof, with roosters and horses running around and a view of the ocean while I chose to work on my farm. Nevertheless, I hadn't said the words, and I hadn't taken action, but everything has its time.

I felt like this was finally the time to make that move.

CHAPTER 13:

VIEQUES

I called up the woman who had approached me at the Denver Salsa Bachata Congress and said that my calendar had opened for 2017 and I was looking for another project. What did she have in mind? She told me to come to Vieques and check it out, so I made plans in January 2017 to go for 6 weeks. This would be my first solo adventure since being paralyzed 5 years earlier, and it was going to be to la Isla Nena, a 24X4 mile island 8 miles off the main island of Puerto Rico. The Municipality of Vieques sent me videos promoting a beautiful dance studio where I could offer my classes. I was vibrating on a high level. Upon arriving, I decided to stay in Vieques. I had found where I needed to be. It was undeniable. My soul stirred.

Three days after I arrived, my host changed her mind about our agreement and wanted me to pay $30 a night for every night I was here. $210 a week for 6 weeks. $1260 in total. Our energies were at an extreme imbalance, and although she was the catalyst through which I arrived in Vieques, I decided that we would not be working together. My plan had been to leave on the 27th of March to go to the Czech Republic to participate in a week long zouk festival, but finances were extremely thin at the time, and although I already had the plane ticket and all access pass for the event purchased, I felt the call to stay in Vieques. I began sleeping in a hammock behind a local farm to table restaurant in their jungle farm. I woke up every morning to a beautiful symphony of flora and fauna, and I knew I was making the right decision.

I was sitting outside the Panaderia Viequense having coffee and toast one morning, writing and drawing the bustling scene in front of me in my journal with fluorescent pens, when an older gentleman approached me and introduced himself as Indio. He asked me 2 or 3 basic questions about myself and immediately gestured to a man who had approached as I'd been distracted, "This is Alex."

I glanced up at the man who was about to change my life and felt an immediate intrigue that I hadn't felt in years. He asked me what I was doing in Vieques. I mentioned that I'm a salsa instructor. "You teach salsa? I dance salsa!" His smile was beautiful, pure joy at the moment. He seemed aware of his own light and the fact that he was alive. There was simply something special about this man. Something rare.

"Ohhh, OK," I teased, "Let's." We exchanged numbers, and I watched him walk away, his broad shoulders erect and relaxed, a tall secure stature. His hands, notably large and strong. He had said he was working with horses that day. I felt something stir but forced myself to look at my notebook before he could even think to turn around to catch me "hating to see him leave but loving to watch him walk away." The last thing I wanted to do was make the wrong decision again and get caught up for years with someone who wasn't who he seemed.

But then, my ex had been exactly who he had seemed. There had been no surprises. It was not his fault for hoodwinking shenanigans. I'd seen him lose his temper at work many times in the year we'd worked together as river guides before we began dating. He'd enter tirades insulting other guides, throwing things, breaking things. These are not your basic red flags. They are clear signs that life with him would be much worse. I'd still signed up knowing that was his style but somehow thinking that his hate wouldn't extend to me. That's not right. I knew it would. I was challenging my endurance with my own belief systems. No matter how I look at the situation, I can't pretend that I didn't know. I had seen the warnings, tucked them back in my mind, and chose to accept a beautiful, kind man who could also be that other very ugly man often. It was the first and only time I'd chosen to do that. It took sharing out loud, outside of my own thoughts, and receiving a slight push from friends, to remember that I didn't need to allow that sort of behavior into my life from anyone ever again. So, if my ex was, in fact, precisely as I had perceived him from the beginning, I couldn't doubt my perceptions nor intuition.

The handsome claimed salsa dancer didn't call, and my attention had been caught by the many moments of salty breezes in shady patches of sunny beaches to notice. I attended a Taino ceremony with my sister Karaya Bibi, a beautiful, kind, creative tattooed Goddess, to receive my name. "Niki Guarinara, The Guardian of Good Spirits." I was in love with Vieques. My soul knew this path. I had dreamed of this as a child. I spoke my thoughts into words in that ceremony. My decision had been made: I would return to Vieques in February and make my home here after I finished my obligations in the United States.

The decision lifted the remaining heaviness from my shoulders. The thoughts I felt in my soul since I was 4 had become words in my early 30s, and now the process had begun to align them with my actions. I continued exploring the island, now with new fervor. I was exploring my home. Two days before my planned departure, my phone rang, and on the other end was a voice I could never forget, though I'd forgotten the name of the caller completely.

"Auria, it's Alex. You remember me?" Ooh! I liked his voice. It sounded familiar. Who had I met that would be calling me with a voice like that? Was this a joke? Then it hit me.

"Alex, *el salsero*! The one in front of the Panaderia?" I was surprised I'd forgotten about him as the days had passed. In those moments, I was in a love affair with myself and had forgotten to look for company beyond Mother Nature and me. He called under the guise of wanting a private lesson. I don't date my students, ever, so I told him that, yes, I'd teach him salsa, but no, as per the rule, I would never date him after. He decided he didn't want a lesson.

The last day I was on the island, we walked in the jungle. I found myself smiling, showing all of my teeth as he pulled samples from fruit trees and vines I hadn't recognized. Taste this. What do you think of that? He was in work boots and jeans; I wore flip flops and running shorts. We swam on the north side of the island, flirting in the ocean, enjoying the conversation. He shared with me his projects and dreams. Told me about his horses. We sat on a rounded volcanic rock shoulder to shoulder, hip to hip, and he turned and kissed me without hesitation.

"F*ck. I'm leaving today," was all I could say the moment our lips parted. I laughed hysterically. He laughed and took me in his arms before looking into my eyes and offering a hand in my descent from the rock. We walked out of the jungle hand in hand and went to the ferry terminal for my departure. We ended up postponing my trip three times until I finally reluctantly boarded the ship to leave la Isla Nena.

We kept in contact for the next 2.5 months while I taught Afro Latin dance classes in Colorado. We began talking about the "wild one" before we'd even made love for the first time. Who was this girl? I was 34, but I felt like I was in high school again. I had never felt like I would feel ready for a child. In fact, I had been told by Knikki that I would never feel ready, that it was something you just did one day. Yet, here I was, for the first time in my life genuinely getting excited about bringing a baby Tarzan into this world feral and strong on a tiny island without stoplights in the middle of the ocean.

In Colorado, I spent the days teaching dance and the evenings drawing. I drew the picture of La Madre that turned into a manifestation of exactly what was to be while teaching dance and "loosely" tying loose ends. I had made myself purchase a plane ticket, but I self handicapped my return to Vieques in other ways. I felt deep in my soul that this was the next move, and as such, there was a low burning fear of the change that threatened to blow into a raging forest fire at the slightest provocation. Not a fear of failure, but of realizing a lifelong dream. Instinctual protection by pushing off our destinies and true callings may be the worst plague of humanity. I postponed thinking about it as the days passed, compartmentalizing it to the area next to my pain, emotional and physical. I did the same with packing for my trip and finding dog care during my absence. I went dancing in Glenwood Springs, CO, the night before my flight. I began presenting my situation to people to see if I could actually make the trip. If I didn't find someone to stay with the pups, I couldn't leave. To my surprise, the first person I asked said yes.

With that covered, I had no excuse left. I caught a ride to the airport with a new resolve to do what my soul knew was the thing I needed to do. I began to allow myself to think about the fact that I was moving to Vieques as I stood in line at the airport to check-in, and I felt as if the entire airport was cheering me on.

When I handed the attendant my identification and flight number, he gave me a puzzled look, "What are you doing here? That flight left at 2:30 PM." I looked at the itinerary in my hand, confused, and there in clear black and white letters was exactly what he had said. The flight was for 2:30PM, not 10:22PM. 10:22PM was the departure for my connecting flight from Miami. I had misread the itinerary more than 100 times in the month since I had bought the ticket. Like most situations when you complain, you could take 5% or so of that energy and fix the problem, so I like to skip the complaining part because it really just wastes time and energy. I asked if I could be switched to another flight, but the ticket had already expired, and they weren't quite in the mood to "Give a sistah a break." So, my only option to keep my momentum was to buy another flight right there at the counter. I offered a debit card that I knew was at a double-digit balance at that moment and flinched involuntarily as he ran it. I crossed my fingers in my pockets as I made the $300 purchase for a new seat on a different flight from Denver to San Juan. To my surprise, my wayoverdrafted account had accepted the additional charge to allow me to return. At least he gave me a $250 discount from what he was trying to charge me.

I arrived in San Juan with the cash I had in my pocket and a small black backpack with a pair of sneakers tied to the outside with a negative number in my bank account. This time I knew how to get to Vieques quickly and cheaply. When I returned, I felt my father cheering me on in the slight whistle of a strong ocean breeze. I swung by the garden and asked the Rasta to hang my hammock while I organized things for my stay. He agreed. I slept swaying in the breeze under the protection of the restaurant roof each night, listening to Coquis and insects in a symphony Beethoven couldn't touch. I knew I'd made the right choice.

CHAPTER 14:

LOVE AND THE STORM

Alex and I reconnected and became inseparable. We went everywhere together, working landscaping, playing on the beach, foraging for food, and taking care of horses while I taught a little salsa and bachata on the side. We camped and fished all night, laughing, dancing, and making love. Two souls reuniting and playing in ecstasy. Every overnight trip, he brought Jaimito, his white stallion with blue eyes and a pink snout, a speckled gray gentle beauty, and Pintito, my painted gelding. My dance community in Colorado had fundraised and sent my terriers to me after they'd attacked and eaten the pet duck of my new friend who'd agreed to watch them, so our pack included 3 horses and two dogs on every adventure.

When Hurricane Maria approached, the entire island went into hiding. We spent the night of Maria's wrath in an empty concrete one-story house in Santa

Maria with a missing door and a window that didn't fully close. There was no furniture in the house. No running water. No electricity. Just us and an air mattress. It was a true "I am home when I'm with you." The living room and bedroom where we were staying flooded. The air mattress floated and lifted off the water when strong gusts funneled into the room. Alex and I lay side by side in silence, my left ear against his chest, feeling for his heartbeat that should have been easy to hear, but with the screaming freight train of Mother Nature's raw power shaking the concrete walls, snapping and tossing entire trees like toothpicks, I could hear nothing. My hand was on his, his was on his bible, rested on his abdomen. I focused on my breath. Alex's strong heartbeat kept my mind vacant and allowed my body to relax. We couldn't talk to each other; it was simply too loud. Firefights in Afghanistan were less noisy than this storm.

When we woke up the next morning, she was still raging. We couldn't open the door to the bedroom until the afternoon. When we opened the front door, we saw that there was no way to leave the driveway with the scooter, so we were on foot. After climbing over stacks of downed trees to get to the main road, our first stop was to the beach to survey the damage, search for useful things, and look for a fresh seafood dinner. We found more than 10 small squids washed up, took them home, and ate like royalty after cooking them on an open fire. The next day we spent the entire day with chainsaws and machetes, clearing our way out of the dirt driveway.

Two days after She passed, I realized that I was pregnant. There was no electricity or running water and zero communication from the island. The ferry wasn't running. The stores weren't open because there was nothing left to buy. Nobody could take any payment but cash, but the bank couldn't open, and ATMs had been empty before the storm even landed. Everyone and everything was looking for a place to live, meaning ticks, fleas, mosquitoes, tarantulas, scorpions, rats, centipedes... everything. Alex and I were helping clear roads, houses, yards, etc. for the next several months, riding around on a borrowed scooter with bad brakes weighed down with his giant frame, our work bag, and me. We had machetes with cardboard folded over their blades, and a chainsaw tied to the back of the seat. Every few minutes there would be a downed tree, piece of a destruction, or a downed light post to navigate, so the ride included a lot of dismounting and mounting. Sometimes we rode Jaimito to work when the scooter wasn't starting well.

It was a faster trip by horse at times than to have to lift a scooter over a downed electric post.

Karaya and I turned to art and dance. It was amazing to see the community come together to function again. Just like in war, we posted all activities on the cork board in the plaza of Isabel II, where lunch plates were served, because everyone needs to eat, everyone needs to check the announcements, and art can pull you through the darkest of places. Although many of us had lost most things tangible, those sweltering September moments were life, too. We could still move. Art and movement filled our days and our hearts. Through sharing salsa classes, Zumba classes, fire spinning, yoga, and art, we could feel Zen in the devastation, the opportunities to rebuild something beautiful. A way to move forward, stronger together. It is art that bonds the pieces of a shattered heart.

On January 7th, more than 3 months later, I woke up in Alex's grandmother's house, where we had been staying since just after Thanksgiving while trying to rebuild our lives to prepare for our baby boy. I was feeling desperate to make a big change. I had no nest to build, and I was due May 28th. I woke up craving a long john, an éclair. Pregnancy cravings take precedence. I thought of my father and his favorite donut when Alex and I got into line to order at La Panaderia Viequense, where it had all started.

There was a group of people having a conversation by the door about advocating for veterans and offering help. Alex overheard and chimed in, letting them know I was a pregnant combat veteran. Their attention shifted to me and I took the opportunity to ask about maybe trading their organization a beat-up trailer that had been tossed around by the hurricane for materials to build a small 12X12 shack on our land before my baby was to be born. They took me outside and asked me some questions while recording a video. That's how I met Ozzy Ramos, Founder and President of the organization, Home of Miracles & Embraces (H.O.M.E.).

The questions he asked me brought to light my combat experience, Purple Heart, paralysis, pregnancy, homeless status, and the complete lack of Veteran health care on the island. He asked how I got to my appointments. I explained that since the VA had referred me to a gynecological clinic in Rio Piedras, I was waking up at 3AM to make it to the ferry terminal by 4 to stand in line to ensure a space on the 6AM boat for my appointment. The ticket window opens at 5, the boat departs at 6 and arrives about 7:40AM. From there, I caught a publico (a 15 passenger van that runs as a taxi) to Rio Piedras for an additional hour and a half ride, so I never could book an appointment before 10AM. The publico would then come to pick me up around 3PM to reverse the process, so I could return before the last ferry. Sometimes we didn't make it to the ferry in time and needed to spend the night in Fajardo to catch it the next morning at 4AM. I explained the cost: only $4 round trip on the ferry but $50 in publicos for the day. Or, $50 in a round trip vehicle pass plus gas. The hotel was $50 for the night as well. Oh, and about 17 hours of a day.

I had appointments every week at that. It was simply not financially possible to maintain that level of spending even if they did reimburse my expenses. It took more than two weeks, sometimes up to a full month, before the money was deposited back in my account.

Ozzy then added something that reminded me of elevator music behind my voice and posted the video on social media. It went viral and was seen by Pedro Smith Blondet in the Pentagon who has a friend, Steven Pauli Simonpietri, who lives in San Juan. Steven is a pilot and a fun, genuinely kind human being. He called and told me that he would like to offer me a free private flight to each of my appointments. He only asked for a day's notice, and in the last month of my pregnancy, there was a possibility that he could be on call. That kindness changed everything about travel to my appointments. Suddenly I could get to an appointment in the morning and be home long before dark. Ten hours of preparation and travel had now dropped to an hour and a half.

A couple days later, I was contacted by a beautiful soul by the name of Erin Schrode, the COO of World Central Kitchen, "Hi, my name is Erin. I have been working here in Puerto Rico for the past four months, and your story just crossed my path. Please don't think I am crazy, but my friend and I have decided that we want to change your life!" she chirped cheerfully. I didn't know how to respond, so I stayed silent. Unhindered, she continued to explain to me how her "Hurricane Husband" Robin Townley and she wanted to help. He ran logistics for a global shipping company and had set up a container home to be built for me. She said that she would be finding us a temporary home on Vieques for the near future and providing us with quality hot meals, any dry foods I needed, and fresh fruit and vegetables for optimal nutrition for the duration of my pregnancy. What else did I need?

I had a hard time sifting through disbelief to find words. What else did I need? I was so used to thriving on the bare minimum. I hesitated. I was nearly moved to tears. I felt a temptation to dare to hope. She repeated her question. What did I need?

- Reliable communication – I hadn't yet been able to get online and reach out to my family.
- A structure on our small piece of land in Verde Vieques Sur, where there are parcels of land that have been returned from the Navy occupation of the island and redistributed among Viequenses.
- Shelter until a home is built
- Energy/Water
- Basic appliances and minimal furniture
- Baby boy…everything
- Tools to work the land
- A pick-up truck to bring building materials and hay to the land
- Starts and seeds to get started on our sustainable garden

A few days later Robin Townley came to Vieques, bringing with him a 5000W generator purchased half by Ozzy Ramos and half by Jason Matos, a new phone, some USB chargers, and a 500W power bank. His first words were, "Are you ready for your life to change? Are you excited?" I hesitated, squinting, scrutinizing. I reserve excitement for things when I know for sure they are happening. While they are happening. Everything still sounded so unrealistic that I couldn't work up excitement. I told him just that.

"I've learned to reserve my reactions for what is happening at this very moment. It keeps me present and staves disappointment when things fall apart."

"Maybe it's time to practice having some faith!" he smiled brightly.

The next week he brought Alex and I to San Juan to pick a design for the hurricane proof container home. It seemed too good to be true. Afterwards we were to have lunch and then meet with Senator Correra to talk about our road situation, since the road to our neighborhood is only accessible by vehicles with all-terrain tires and 4X4. No cement trucks, the municipal water truck, nor the garbage truck can make it up the hill to our neighborhood. When it storms, the safest method to get off the hill is on foot. The senator vaguely promised to see what he could do, and I knew in my gut that it wouldn't happen as I smiled stiffly for the camera.

The road wasn't going to be fixed by that senator, but the things that Erin had promised to do, she did immediately or enabled us to do ourselves. When I met her, I had met a sister. She had a blender in hand, ready to help me make fruit juices in the morning. I found myself jumping up and down, screaming with excitement. Fresh juice after the hurricane. She found us a temporary housing fix and paid for it out of her own pocket for 6 months. World Central Kitchen then gave us a generous stipend to use at Placita Reyes, the visiting fresh food stand, so we could eat healthily again. Then Erin encouraged me to fill out a Plow to Plate grant from World Central Kitchen to move forward with Alex and my dream of farming and living one with the land in a sustainable way. I had wanted to create a farm to plate relationship with my family, my local community, and restaurants here in Vieques. I included the tools to work the land, the pickup truck, and the stars and seeds in the grant paperwork, and was awarded the funds to purchase these items.

Fundacion Janet Arce sent us a 16 in. chainsaw to help us work on the land. She organized for a baby shower drop off in Fajardo. Lucy Santos came to Vieques with Gina Sein on their own dime and hand delivered an entire baby shower worth of gifts for David. Zorimar Betancourt came to Vieques represen-ting Fundacion Stefano Steenbakkers Betancourt accompanied by Rooms To Go Puerto Rico and donated a functional washing machine and everything I could possibly think of needing from their warehouse.

I had started to believe that the container home might actually be built as well, as Robin seemed genuinely excited about the planning process. He discussed the logistics of getting containers up our hill with me. Chinooks or cranes. It all seemed to make the idea more and more plausible. I felt more and more hopeful, until mid-February when he suddenly stopped returning my text messages. Having been the director of a dance festival, I recognized the behavior pattern nearly immediately, and it made my stomach turn. It's the behavior of someone who hasn't learned the simple skill of adult communication when a mistake has been made. I continued to tag him on social media and text him updates without avail. He had swooped in like a hero and promised something he couldn't deliver, but instead of talking to me about it like a grown man, he began to avoid me like a teenage soon to be ex-boyfriend.

It was the last week of March when I finally was able to find out what had happened through Erin Schrode, who texted him to ask about the progress of the home for me. He responded to her, not to me. He'd promised to help using company resources before even presenting my story to the company. The

$50,000 estimated cost that he claimed had already been paid had actually not even been approved. How much had "his people" raised privately? About $2,600.

I was not shocked. I found myself disappointed because I had finally begun to "have some faith" against my intuition, but by the time Erin gave me the secondhand answer, it was just confirmation of something I already knew in my gut since the first moment I'd met Robin. The container home sounded too good to be true, and so it was. We'd have a little boost in cash to buy some building materials though, and for that I was thankful.

I called Ozzy again to drop the news. I was feeling the pressure to nest, my son would be arriving in 2 months, and the promise of this house had stopped us in our tracks and redirected us. Now we had lost 6 weeks of preparation, I felt more than a bit lost. David's due date was nearing. Ozzy Ramos and H.O.M.E. began a fundraiser for the "Soon to be homeless 7-month pregnant Purple Heart and combat veteran after Hurricane Maria." I didn't like asking for donations. It didn't feel natural asking for help.

CHAPTER 15:

DAVID ALEXIS

When I woke up on Sunday, April 8th, 2018, I felt strong waves of back pain and thought, "Hmm, is this how early labor feels?" David's due date was May 28th, so I didn't want to be in labor. I relaxed, drank a ton of water, and began timing my contractions in denial as they became shorter and shorter. By 3PM, there was enough blood for me to tell Alex that it was time to go to the hospital. Within 10 minutes, we arrived at the non-sterile medical tent, where the doomsday gynecologist, who smelled like alcohol, couldn't stop repeating how both David and I would be in bad shape, damaged, etc., because I was only 33 weeks pregnant. He was telling everyone to prepare for the worst after they searched for the incubator, which was unprepared, still in pieces, and for which they couldn't find the cord. They then made the executive decision to do precisely what they should have done since the beginning and fly me to the hospital on the main island. After an additional ambulance ride from Centro Medico to Presbyteriano in Condado, they prepared me for childbirth. For some reason, they were having Alex wait outside. However, Señor Negativity is still there, telling me how damaged my child will be and not to expect anything too good.

Eventually, I looked him in his eyes and told him two things:

1. That's not what you are supposed to tell me, bro.
2. My child WILL be healthy. Back off, you are not scaring me.

After a while, my requests turned into demands for Alex's presence. I wore them down, and he was brought into the room. That's when it happened. The doctor realized that my water had broken from the top, not from the bottom, and chose to break it manually.

The moment she broke the sack of fluid, she announced frantically, "His feet are coming! Emergency C-Section!" Then looks at Alex and me accusingly, "The doctor didn't tell you he wasn't in position?"

Before I had a chance to point out that she just had her hand in my vagina, feeling the baby's position before breaking the sack, I was being rushed to another room. I watched the rectangular fluorescent lights pass as they pushed me down the hospital hallway at a run. I felt calm. I wondered if I'd live through this or if these were my last living memories. I was wiped down and told to count backward from 10. Sedated. 4 hours later, I woke up to a nurse carefully explaining, "So, uh, we had some complications during your surgery. Your baby is fine, but we cut open your bladder. The urologist sewed it back up, and now you are in observation."

"Wait, you what?" This can't be real.

Apparently, David was screaming, "I do what I want," as he tried to kick his way to freedom from my womb. He even managed to get his feet out to the knees before they forced him back inside to exit in a more acceptable manner. I'm proud of him for already breaking social norms. Declaring that he will live life on his own terms, for although he came physically through me, this is his life.

David Alexis Abreu Maldonado was born at 5:50PM Sunday, April 8th, at 4lbs 15 oz, already a miracle and ready to become a warrior. I wasn't allowed to see my son that night because visiting hours in the NICU begin in the morning, and I couldn't get my scalpel-ravaged torso to bend into a wheelchair hours after being sliced open. He spent a full month in the Neonatal Intensive Care Unit until he weighed 5 solid lbs. While he was chubbing up and developing more strength to breathe, I was receiving treatment for my bladder that had been lacerated during the procedure. I had been told by the urologist that my doctor had made the mistake because she had been confused by the appearance of my neurogenic bladder. An organ whose walls are usually 3 millimeters thick was now over a centimeter thick in my life post rat lungworm. He recommended that I start medication that obviously wouldn't be healthy for my breastfed premature baby. I declined.

The morning after I gave birth, Alex looked at me with a mischievous twinkle in his eye and said, "Okay, you ready to have the girl now?" Perhaps it was the hormones, but I immediately began sobbing and felt a pressing fear. I shook my head, thinking of how my entire life, I felt as if I would die in childbirth, and I was still alive after that crazy ordeal with David Alexis. Those memories hadn't been my last. Now, for the first time at 35, after 2 years in combat, I felt a foreign fear of death. That translated to for the first time in my entire life, I'd never had a true reason to live. I was living, not just existing, but I didn't have a genuine reason to need to stay breathing, and so risks were just another thing. It all began to make sense to me why I signed up for the dangerous missions, jumped out of planes, totaled cars, and climbed up waterfalls. Suddenly, those sorts of activities weren't options, not because I had a lacerated bladder, nor because the danger level had changed, but because I had a distinct reason not to want to take the risks I had once needed. I had been given the opportunity to raise an entire human being. What an immense treasure!

When we came back to Vieques in May, we were still living in the beautiful little yellow house. Our lease was ending on the 22nd of July, and they were going to raise the rent an additional $750 because the house was for tourists and the love of money making, not locals with newborns, so we were back on our own. We moved our tribe up to the land closer to our project: our farm and the house. We set up in a 9x9ft tent. Every day I was propagating herbs, and Alex was building our home. Some days he had his friend Indio to help him, other times he worked alone. His cousin Manuel even came up one day to place blocks, and my uncle Edwin Borrero came to Vieques to meet me and help as well. We were able to purchase most of the building materials for the foundation with the donations raised by H.O.M.E. After that, Steven, the amazing pilot I keep mentioning, donated $500 worth of cinder blocks to help us finish the walls. The deal was I'd work on developing the farm, and he'd build the house, and we'd help each other. Our dream was to build a house on the hill disconnected from the madness and raise our children organically, as ones with the Earth.

We worked tirelessly together on our dream. When tires exploded, we brought water up our hill by hand in whatever we had. Sometimes it was 5-gallon buckets. We traded off carrying David's car seat and buckets of water. Each evening we heated water and bathed with a 5-gallon bucket of water and a cup on a piece of wood from the construction after having dinner while watching the sun set over the ocean. We laid next to our baby and told stories until he drank his milk and fell asleep in my arms, and I returned him to his bassinet, securely covered by a mosquito net. We listened to salsa, insects, birds of the night, and the soft breathing of our son. We watched the stars and pointed out shapes of animals in the passing clouds to the light of the moon. We loved each other, and rather quickly, I found that I was pregnant a second time.

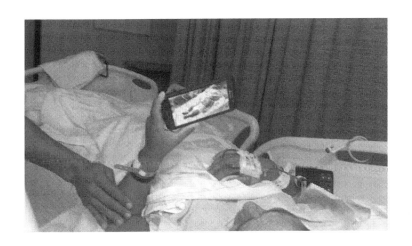

CHAPTER 16:

I LOVE YOU TO INFINITY

In November, I was contacted by my friend Sid Moffatt from Haines, Alaska. She was coming to San Juan on November 24th via cruise ship and asked if I wanted to meet up in the morning so she could meet Baby David Alexis? Absolutely.

We were sipping coffee, laughing freely, when I received a call from Alex. He told me he was walking in the sun in Carolina. He sounded tired and down, which was uncharacteristic. He said something inaudible, and when I asked him to repeat himself, he told me that he loved me. Five times he repeated himself.

"I love you to infinity. Take a seat in the shade." I mentioned I was having coffee in Old San Juan. He told me he loved me to infinity and would call me later. We hung up. Those were the last words I'd ever hear him say to me.

It wasn't until nearly 7:30 PM that I received the call. His cousin called me crying, slurring her words in uncontrollable sobs. I immediately knew what she was going to tell me. I reserved all breaths, reactions, comments, and thoughts until I had stepped back and braced myself against the wall. The man I'd chosen and who had chosen me, the only man with whom I've ever even truly desired to share my life and home, to have children with and raise a family, was dead. He'd had a heart attack, with nobody by his side. Someone was close enough to rob his cash and take his phone with so many beautiful pictures of us before the paramedics arrived, just not to lift a finger to save his life.

I went straight to the emergency room of UPR, where the police had told me I needed to go to identify Alex's body. When I arrived, a sweet-faced young doctor sat me down in a corner office of the emergency room and stuttered awkwardly through my notification of my partner's death. I sat, staring blankly while he struggled with his words. No tears. No fighting. Just silence. He didn't know how to handle such a calm receipt of such horrific news. He assured me that they had attempted to revive him for over 40 minutes. Alex's ribs must be cracked under the pressure of 40 minutes of CPR. He was sorry. So very sorry for my loss. I was 19 weeks pregnant and had a 7.5-month-old clone of his father waiting outside in the car with my sister Ita. Just like that, there were not going to be any more kisses on my belly morning, noon, and night. No more, "Good morning, my love," first thing each day. No more deep rumbling laugh with his lips pressed against my neck, his stubble scratching me and making me squirm away, displaying my dimple in schoolgirl giggles.

He hadn't finished the house. There were still no windows, doors, porch, shower, or bathroom. The 4x4 pickup truck I was using to go up and down the hill to the property had a blown engine, and now the love of my life and father of my children was gone. I stayed until 3AM waiting for a chance to identify his body, for the moment when we would take the elevator down to the morgue, and I could tell them with certainty that they had the wrong guy, but that chance never came. My status changed at that moment to homeless combat veteran, widow, and pregnant single mother of a 7-month-old boy.

I got back to my sister's house in Bayamon at nearly 5AM. I wasn't even close to ready to try to lay down and allow my mind the freedom to ravage me in my dreams. I have been the only person who's heard all my thoughts my entire life, and I needed to write them out to Alex. I was the obviously pregnant grieving woman who couldn't seem to stop the tears from flowing no matter how slowly and calmly she breathed. I had nobody that I wanted to talk to. That's different than having nobody to talk to. Isolation. I just wanted to hug and hold myself and spend time with my son without having any conversations to satisfy prodding curiosity into my grief poorly masked as concern. The afternoon after Alex's death, I wrote to him:

November 25th '18

Alex,

You died yesterday at 1:48 PM, the exact moment that I'd sent a text to Ita saying that you'd called. The emptiness I feel is stark. It is lonely. I haven't slept yet. It's nearly 5 PM. I imagine I will fall asleep soon, but what's the point if when I wake up, I must face the fact that you are already on a cold metal slab, nearly frozen and very dead.

I'm struggling with wanting to continue without you. What…HOW did you have a heart attack? How did you stop breathing? How did nobody touch you until the paramedics showed up? HOW IS THAT F*CKING POSSIBLE? You were already dead when the ambulance arrived, but they tried to revive you for over 40 minutes. You died while I had coffee with Sid. You took your last breath after calling me to say goodbye. We did everything together, yet you died alone, with nobody by your side to try to save your life. All the love we have for one another, and you died alone, 20 minutes from me while I made light jokes with my friend over lattes.

I didn't even receive the call to go to the hospital until you were already dead for over 6 hours. SIX HOURS!!! "I love you to infinity!" My last words to you on this side of the veil.

I loved you. I love you. I will love you, and I will love your children. They will know how much their daddy loved them. How we made so many plans. They will know everything about what a beautiful man you were. How you worked your ass off for them. They will know your adventurous spirit and your sense of humor; How you asked me over and over if I'd fit between cars when I had our daughter growing in my belly.

They will see all the videos we have. Well, most. Some of them aren't for their eyes.

I miss you. I don't know what to do without you. I am completely lost. Desperately lost at this moment. You are always in my thoughts. You have been since the first day we spent together.

I love you more than I can express. I don't understand the rules. The Universe has been so damn hard on me. When a teacher seems unfairly harsh, it is usually dismissed with the explanation of "seeing untapped potential." This I don't understand. Goddammit! I wanted to grow old with you! Planting, adventuring, foraging, traveling, living. LIVING. Walking beaches, finding caracoles, celebrating life…watching clouds. ALIVE! Finding hearts together. LAUGHING! I love you. That will never change.

I miss you so much already. HOW DO I DO THIS? I want my son to know you. You were so excited to watch David ride his first horse that you held him on a goat at 3 months old. So excited for him to work that he already has a tiny pickaxe waiting for him that he won't be able to touch for MANY years. THIS IS NOT FAIR! I want him to know his father, for Auria to know her father! You were supposed to be with us forever!

I miss everything about you, even the way you chew.

I love you to infinity.

The grief, all-consuming in moments, left me sputtering and choking through the deepest swells where all I could do was allow it to wash over me in a tsunami-esque wave and cling for my life until it receded slightly. I wrote to Alex in the morning and evening as if he was on deployment or traveling because that's the only way I could function. He was on another adventure, about which I know not. I didn't judge myself. My soul said I needed to continue communicating with him, and that was the only thing that made sense. When I finished a letter, I signed off with "I love you to infinity," just like we always said. I felt his energy in the soft caress of wind behind my ears, the way the morning sun rested gently on my cheeks.

Everybody wanted to talk about how he died, but I wanted to talk about how he lived. He was still alive within me, and I saw him clearly in my child's eyes, so I had no desire to see anyone else. I was more lost than I'd ever been in my life, and finally, I recognized that I needed help. I noticed on Facebook that my friend Claudia Benjamin, a Milton Hershey School student with whom I had lived, and therefore my sister, had created a GoFundMe. I wrote this plea through tears for help to pay for the funeral expenses, purchase a vehicle to get up and down our 4x4 adventure driveway, and finish the house with any extra funds:

November 26th '18

Many of you have asked me how you can help during this unfathomable challenge while my soul is shattered and my head feels permanently submerged with my heart in this torrent of tears. Many have pleaded with me to ask for help.

My pride was swept away completely by sudden, incomprehensible tragedy.

I'm broke… and broken...

I NEED HELP...

I am, for the first time in my life, completely and utterly lost...without direction... without motivation... without a clue how to handle any of this.

My soul life partner and best friend has died.

All three of my dogs have died.

Someone stole my goats (I plan to find them).

My tent was ransacked.

#babydavidalexis giggles and grabs the phone when he recognizes his father's voice, while my heart and throat throb in unison.

I have no reliable transportation.

My meaningless but helpful worldly possessions are split between multiple locations....

I have a 7.5 month old boy and I'm 19 weeks pregnant with his little sister.

This is the hardest situation I've faced to date...

Worse than war.

Worse than firefights & losing friends.

Worse than an IED blast.

Worse than my father's suicide.

Worse than being paralyzed by rat lungworm.

Worse than pregnancy 2 days after Hurricane Maria.

Worse than my homelessness.

I need to bury the man I chose...who chose me. I must accept that my daughter #babyauriaalexandra will never get to genuinely feel her father's loving embrace...and I still need to finish a house.

Please help me put this magnificent, talented soul to rest next to his beautiful mother. Any extra funds collected shall go towards a vehicle and the construction of the house for our children.

This is my official cry for help.

It took forensics 25 full days to release the body of the father of my children. That meant that on December 19th, 2018, my 36th birthday, 6 years after I had franken-walked out of the hospital, I had the opportunity to spend the entire day with the decomposing body of my love, to truly see that he was gone. On those days, I wrote these letters to him.

December 19th '18 afternoon

Alex,

It's my birthday. They brought you for my birthday. This is the absolute hardest thing I've ever experienced in my life. Luckily, there are plenty of women here who want to hold and play with David, so I have this free moment to write to you. When we woke up this morning, David was running a bit of a fever, but he seems to be his normal cheerful, energetic self. He looks so much like you. I know you said he looks like me when he's asleep, but I'd rather him look like you.

I received your message today from your friend in Bayamon while I was parked at the beach waiting to hear that your body had arrived at your grandmother's house. I know you love me. I know you'll always be with us… and I will continue our dream. The young boy with light-colored hair will be raised on the hill like in your dream, and he will have a small fruit tree by the door like we planned. He will protect his little sister and his mother like you always told him. We know you love us.

Let's talk about what they did to your body. First, it's been 25 days, and this is obvious because of your hands. They are deeply wrinkled. They look cold, and they are the wrong color… like maybe they were frozen for 25 days then thawed to be shoved into a tight suit, then a box, and put on display in a house in the tropics without air conditioning for 24 hours. Imagine that. I want to grab them and not let go until they are warm again. How I loved those hands.

The makeup they put on you is the wrong color, and the smell is ridiculous. They put makeup inside your nose and in your beard. Now it is caked and ugly. There's something wrong with your right eye, and God knows they messed up your lips. They put obvious eyeliner on you… I mean obvious, and the tar-like makeup from your hair got on the tips of your ears.

They put you into a super uncomfortable-looking suit that has bits of makeup on it everywhere, and the pillow is too thick, forcing your chin down towards your neck. You look extremely uncomfortable. I don't know exactly how they messed up your mouth, but it appears that you are frowning slightly, like how you do involuntarily when you are trying to see something on your clavicle.

You are wearing a baseball cap. I've never once seen you in a hat like that. Ah yes, they threw it at the last minute to hide the fact that they sawed open your skull, I guess. Sawed open your skull, sliced open your chest, then shoved you into a box too small before deciding to upgrade you (for free! Wow! What a gift!) to a bigger casket.

I'm sorry for my sarcasm. None of this is fair. None of it.

I've been here, by your side since 12:30 PM. It's now 3 AM, and I finally feel that I'm tired enough to at least lay down and dream with you.

Please come visit me in my dreams.

I love you to infinity.

December 20th

It's not morning.

It is mourning.

I spent my birthday yesterday with you. I was with you from 12:40 PM until 3AM.... fell asleep... then 6AM... until I collapsed onto your body before they closed your casket... at 12:30PM today... begging you to find me... promising to find you... and couldn't take my hand from it until it was out of my reach... I rode with you to the cemetery... and I saw the heart clouds... While you were being buried, I took turns between frantically searching the sky for more proof your soul didn't accompany your body into the ground and fighting valiantly against my urge to throw myself into the hole and be buried with you. I stood dangerously close on the off chance that maybe the digger dude would slip and help me out. I stayed until I was ushered off the gravesite by my ride... being that we were the last ones left. I went to get my rig, and now I'm back at your plot because this is the one place I believe I should be. I've been repeating the same phrase since you were first lowered into the ground, and now, I'll ask you in black and white, WHAT THE F*CK DO I DO NOW!? I'm so utterly lost.

Please speak to me today.

I love you to infinity.

December 20th '18 afternoon

Alex,

Hello, my love. I don't know what to do now. I'm sitting by your grave. You are six feet underground... and I'm alone sitting on the dirt by your grave. I woke up at 6 AM. I spent the entire day with you.

You must have seen my last-ditch attempt at getting you to find me, connect with me on the other side. I couldn't take my hands from the casket until it was moved out of my reach. Marlon invited me to ride with you in the hearse from your grandmother's house to the cemetery. I know I will never have the liberty to forget that smell. I just needed to take one last ride with you. I needed to be near you.

Alex, help me. I don't know the map. I don't know what step to take. I don't know where to go. *Pa'lante* means absolutely nothing to me. I'm broken…Yet my body continues to function. MAKE IT MAKE SENSE! The autopsy report is still not finished. I NEED TO KNOW WHY YOU DIED AT 41 WHEN THERE ARE OLD CAREER ALCOHOLICS AND CRACK HEADS HANGING ON THE CORNER DAILY!!

I'm so hurt. The breeze feels nice, but my eyes hurt. My nose hurts. My butt hurts (I'm sitting on some hard ground). You brought a bunch of heart clouds to the ceremony. I'm pretty sure I'm the only one who saw them. I love us, Alex. We had our moments, but I could easily spend multiple lifetimes by your side as *"La Mujer de Alex," "La esposa de Alex,"* You know…Her.

I had a problem not having my individual identity here at first, then I grew proud of the title. You really are one of a kind. I will love you forever. Now they call me "the widow with two babies." That doesn't have nearly the ring of "*La'posa d'Alex.*" I miss your hands, your traps. Your strength. Your laugh. God, how I miss your laugh. I love that you were always so silly. I miss you always telling me I'm beautiful. I miss you complimenting my a** and my mind.

Why did you leave? Your autopsy results have not been brought yet.

(Your daughter just moved in my belly.) 26 days after your death, there is still no death certificate because there is no autopsy? I need to have a mission. I must stay busy to even be close to O.K. right now. My disability claim through the VA is being rushed because I'm officially a "homeless veteran," whatever that means. Home is not a place, it is when I am with my family. It's where I feel comfortable. I would feel more lost in a mansion in Puerto Rico than in our tent on our hill in Vieques.

I hate this cemetery. It's unkempt. You have to have a simple cross for a year before a headstone is allowed, and many graves appear to have been forgotten by families and "loved ones" who lack patience. There are horses stepping on everyone and patches of scraggly grass growing sporadically throughout. There is no pathway on which to walk without getting covered in mud when it rains. Please, don't leave me. While I was writing this, four hearts appeared in the sky with a silhouette of a *jibaro*. It made me begin to whistle *El Caballo Viejo*.

I love you to infinity.

What the f*ck do I do now?

I struggled. I remembered moments I could have been kinder to him, and I felt him forgive me. I felt him apologize. I felt his pain. I found signs of his love everywhere; heart shapes appeared in everything. I knew he hadn't abandoned us. I watched David play with him most mornings through tears. I could not consider a day as a block of time during these days. It was down to the very moment. When someone asked me the dreaded question, "How are you?" I had to break it down to the very moment, "In this moment I'm..." to be honest. I hate that question.

I missed the man who danced with me everywhere. If a good salsa came on, it didn't matter if we were outside or inside, in a restaurant or at the grocery store, he would grab my hand, slide his hand around my waist, and dance with me. I adored the faces he made while he followed the clave. His lips pursed playfully in agreement with a good break. Always smiling radiantly.

He visited me one day at the land to have a last dance, and I wrote to him that night:

January 13th

Alex,

I went to the land as soon as the mechanic finished today and did some propagation of herbs. While I was there, it began to rain torrentially. I didn't have an extra set of clothes with me, so before I got too wet, I stripped down, put my clothes in the car to stay dry, and let the rain refresh and renew as we have done many times together. It was quite magnificent... and for the first time since you left, for a beautiful moment, I felt unadulterated joy fill my broken heart. I felt you slide your hand around my waist. I felt your hand in my hand. My tears fell freely as I laughed, drinking in a flood of Universal love. I felt *Pacha Mama. Atabey.* Mother Earth and I laughed hysterically while I spun barefoot and naked in the mud. How Grounding. I felt love. I felt a connection. I felt hope. And I felt the goo between my toes. I must have looked crazy, but that's a tiny price to pay to dance in the rain with you one more time.

I love you to infinity.

236

CHAPTER 17:

AURIA ALEXANDRA

Alex being gone left a gaping hole in me that I simply didn't know how to fill. The morning after he passed away, his "family" came up our hill and stole my goats, Jaimito (his white stallion), and his saddle. My terriers that I had brought with me from the United States had both passed away that week, and our new puppy had been hit by a tourist. I found myself screaming to the Universe, cursing life, sad, angry, and yet there was a baby looking to me to giggle with him about everything. Not just a baby, but the man who had changed my world like no other and had awakened within me an emotion that I never quite knew to exist; something raw, pure, and beautiful. Love in its most naked form. My Wild One, my *Salvajito*, was there saving my life with his presence when I doubted if I wanted to continue. He wiped my tears and gave me a clear reason, along with his sister kicking in my belly to survive when I felt I, too, should cross the veil and bask in the unmarred light of my lover once more.

I didn't know what I was doing. I just knew that the last thing I'd ever want him or his sister to feel is as if they are burdens. It is for their sake that I would stay and live these moments until I could find it in my soul to live for my sake as well. So mid sob, I'd find myself smiling at my son. The juxtaposition of two emotions is so different, but so connected. Tragedy and Beauty. Joy and sorrow. The cycle of life. New life makes losing life easier to comprehend.

Vieques is a small island, and the news traveled fast about my situation. Kind souls and a few non-profit organizations stepped in immediately to assist me. For that, I will be forever grateful. First, Kalina, the owner of Jurutungo Tours sent me a message. She offered me a room in her house free of charge and a place to keep Jaimito for a while, although we didn't know each other incredibly well. In fact, her exact words had been, "I don't know if you remember me, but you and Alex stopped in front of my house one time looking for a cup of grain to catch a horse." She was clear that I was welcome, my son was welcome, and there was no judgment, just support. I moved in on Christmas day and will be eternally grateful for the privacy she granted me to deal with the most savage beginning stages of grief in her house. I stayed there from Christmas day until the end of February when I moved back up to the 9x9' tent on the land to begin again to work on Alex and my dream. Mark Martin contacted me and had Vieques Love rent me a jeep to get up and down my hill for a week while I organized everything in the tent and dealt with all the paperwork and tasks related to having a partner die.

Marion Fisher from Serenity Point Yoga offered to host a bachata brunch to raise money for my cause and gave me an opportunity to teach a class dedicated to my yearning soul. I almost declined. How can one rise from a torment so cruel to offer light energy and movement for others? But in the darkest storm of my life, the only movement that truly made sense was Afro-Latin. I needed to dance in the rain again, and so I accepted and taught a beginner bachata class on the front porch of her beautiful white ocean front house. A position from which I could see where my love had been buried. The cemetery entrance is right next to the house.

For the second time since Alex passed away, I felt the weight of grief lift from my shoulders and hover patiently in the space held by movement, music, and laughter. I could feel him smiling and enjoying the

239

show and remembered how much he would talk about how I couldn't stop smiling while dancing. It has indeed been my chosen form of effective therapy since 2005. It was February 2nd, 2019, a little over 2 months after Alex crossed the veil, yet for a few hours that early afternoon, I felt like the woman brimming with happiness I once was. I'd missed my best friend and her energy, and I knew when I felt her again in full pregnant hurricane force that day that everything was going to be okay.

Marion and her crew of amazing ladies had planned a surprise baby shower for me for Auria Alexandra, and my volunteer pilot, now friend, Steven showed up with his wife from San Juan to support! I guess when you have a plane, you can do things like that. After our lesson, I was surprised with gifts and donations from all who attended. One gift in particular made me break out in ugly sobs in front of the entire group. It was a newborn onesie. Something super cute, but with a superman S (obviously superwoman in this case), and it said the words, "Strong like Mommy."

Hope Builders contacted me in the following weeks to help me finish building the house. A volunteer from Canada, Josh Krug, had heard my story and sought me out to help me as his last project in Vieques before heading to the Bahamas. Two months after we buried

Alex, Josh told me he would voluntarily build the house. All I needed to do was pick him up at dawn from Santa Maria, provide him with any extra materials he needed beyond what Hope Builders was providing, and bring him back to where he was staying as the sun set, working 12 hours a day. Hope Builders provided all the tin roof, windows, doors, and wood to finish up the house, and I used the GoFundMe funds to purchase the rest. Two weeks later, boom, I had a house for my children and only needed to finish up a bathroom and a shower.

Next, I contacted Edgar Oscar Ruiz, Co-Founder, President & Executive Director of Sail Relief Team because I had heard that he installed solar power systems. I asked for a quote. I received enough funds in the fundraiser to pay for Alex's funeral, purchase a vehicle that could go up and down the hill, and provide all extra materials that Josh requested to finish the house. Aside from that, a little money remained, and I was thinking of ways to invest it to have renewable electricity.

Oscar is an Army veteran as well. He was a combat medic and as such is my brother for life. When he heard that I was a veteran newly widowed with babies and no electricity, he began looking for ways to provide the system less expensively. A few days later, he sent me a message that they had the solar panels, and he'd fundraised the rest of the money towards the 2000W system. What a blessing! He brought groups of volunteers over to help me with everything from throwing the concrete floor with Josh and helping paint the inside of the house to filling tires for a retaining wall so my house didn't slide down the hill with the next tropical storm.

When the time was nearing to go to Condado to give birth to Auria Alexandra Abreu Maldonado, I pulled Oscar aside and asked if he would be okay staying with my vehicle and coming to my land twice a day to feed and water the animals. This sounds like a small task, but really it is not. There were 2 dogs, 2 goats, a horse, and 2 goslings. He obliged easily, telling me that the plan was to install my solar system while I was in the hospital, so when I came home with my daughter, I'd have electricity for a refrigerator and could keep perishable foods in the house with me.

When I went to the main island of Puerto Rico to give birth to my daughter, a calm energy came over my soul. I was going to meet my daughter. Like my adventure race in Costa Rica, I was more than a little bit surprised that I was the only one in the waiting room alone. Everyone else had a husband, boyfriend, family or a friend by their side to help them stand, sit, drink coffee, grab snacks, or carry bags. I had a beautiful friend named Pacha with me, but she was with David Alexis because children are not allowed in that section of the hospital. I had an appointment for 10AM, but they didn't take me back until the late afternoon. By then, my other support system, Liz Zivic, had arrived to take a shift with Pacha and my baby boy.

When the anesthesiologist told me that she would sedate me, I cried. I had been under the impression that I would stay awake throughout the surgery but since I had survived meningitis with remaining neuropathy, the doctor told me she couldn't allow me to stay awake without possibly injuring me further. The temptation to slip away to be with Alex was strong, but the reality of leaving these beautiful children behind broke my heart. I simply could not fathom it. The staff at the hospital was mostly the same as in the past year. They all remembered Alex and me from David's birth, so I had to explain to several nurses and a few doctors that Alex had transitioned. Yes, he was young. Yes, he seemed healthy. I wish he was here to hold his daughter.

Auria was born healthy at 6:52PM on April 15th, exactly one year and one week after her brother. She was 6 lbs 10 oz., 20 inches, and absolutely beautiful.

The experience was different than with her brother. I was in and out of the hospital in 3 quick days with a healthy, beautiful baby girl and no bladder lacerations.

We returned to Vieques and picked up Knikki Cinocco the first evening back. She had come from Alaska to be by my side for the first postpartum weeks with my new daughter. Her love had also been called for his next adventure, and so we grieved together. She was one of the very few I truly invited into my world to trust with my grief, as I knew that she understood, completely, without judgment. That was a time of absolute tragedy and beauty. Sobbing nights filled with hopeful regret. I was constantly trying to adjust my thoughts as I had gotten so skilled at doing but not always successfully.

One day shortly after Knikki returned to Alaska, I spent the morning going down a rabbit hole. When I recognized the pattern, I grabbed a moment to change my situation and location. I loaded the babies quickly in the car and went to The *Finca de Hamberto*, Oscar's farm project created as a hub for eventual food resilience and sustainability education. I pulled up to the volunteer house, and he came out to greet me.

"I was going down a rabbit hole, and I felt that I needed to be around people, so I came here. Is that okay?" I didn't need to ask. I knew it was okay because he's a combat vet, but it's polite to say the words. He told me to stay as long as I wanted and come as often as I liked. In fact, he encouraged me to stay at their farm and do the work at my house while sleeping, eating, and showering there, but I couldn't drum up the desire to separate myself from my mission enough to want to spend nights and mornings elsewhere. I wanted to be in my little house on the hill with my babies, basking in the healing, nonjudgmental energy of *la Madre Tierra, Atabey*. Plus, Alex's energy wasn't at his farm. It's at mine. He understood, but even if he hadn't, my decisions didn't need to make sense to anyone but me. It's my journey, my healing, and I am the only one who knows my true thoughts, so how could somebody else decide what I need to do for me?

I continued to visit the farm, plant seeds, and teach my babies about nature, although it seemed as if they'd always known. They walk among wild plants like old friends catching up on highlights of the years apart. A taste of this, a nibble of that. Just like their father had the first day we spent together and every day after that.

Their father. I was raised with my father. My daughter was never going to have the chance to meet hers. How could I accept that?

Time doesn't stop and wait for you to accept anything. It continues. My *Taino* name is "Niki Guarinara," Guardian of the Good Spirits. I had received my good spirits, and I am their guardian, as they remain my saviors, the single tether to which I desperately clung while struggling to find air as waves of grief batted me around like a discarded soda bottle. A discarded bottle, cracked but unbroken. Filled with a message of hope and love. On her first birthday, I wrote this letter to my daughter:

Auria Alexandra,

To the woman of my dreams, the lady of my heart… She has given life to my existence as the mother of a warrior princess. I am beyond proud to be here to walk our paths together. When I was downtrodden without the energy to eat, I felt your love in my belly, and I ate for you. When I wanted to drown my sorrow in a bottle, I stayed sober for you. When life pushed me beyond my breaking point, I became flexible like never before, for your blood coursed through my veins. You gave me strength. Your heartbeat within me, doubling the speed of my own. Reminding me that new life makes losing life easier to understand…and accept. Your smile…

your eyes, so much like mine, remind me that you are always watching. Always learning. You inspire me to be a better woman to, in turn, inspire you to do the same. You, my nature baby, are love: naked, raw, and honest. Happy first trip around the sun. Thank you for this year of growth, acceptance, and motherhood.

I love you beyond infinity.

It had still not gotten easier to navigate through the waves of grief, though the calm waters between them lengthened slightly. It was as if my sanity sat on a bulging levy that held back compartmentalized anger. No...fury, yearning, emptiness, and loss. Sometimes something as light as an off-colored feather or comment could break it open, leaving me grasping for the present, drowning in lamentations of lost joy... Grief defined is joy lost. I cried for the physical loss of something full of immense joy.

People like to use "You can't pour from an empty cup" as a mantra for self-care. My cup has been burned, scalded, cracked, broken, glued, glazed, and set in the kiln once more, to be set ablaze and become whole once again. It is from this same cup that I shall continue to drink the infinite joyous beauty and inspiration that comes from watching our children grow and choose their paths.

These two beautiful beings I have by my side are the new generation, genetically charged. Brimming with ancestral wisdom undamped. These children offer glimpses of spirits freed through their own curiosity. Their eager eyes hunger for more; more connection. More knowledge. More language. More experiences.

They have not had the privilege to spend physical time in this life with their father or their grandfathers. Yet these spirits stay with us. They ride the wind's soft whisper and howl with joy when she whips through treetops, batting leaves playfully in a sultry rumba celebrating what is because of what has been. They tickle the back of our necks when we ponder the uncanny, a reminder that all is possible. They are the grounding current of the storm that courses our veins and connects us all to everything around us. Our most basic life force. As they light our way, we can find them in the first warm rays of dawn that caress our upturned faces as easily as in the wild nature of the ocean. Constant movement. Constant change. They are with whom we hold space when we are truly present. *La conga, el ritmo en clave* that catches our spirit and leads the beautiful dance through tragedy.

Connection. Fertile Earth and instinctive movement. Dirt, blood, and mud. They are in everything we do. In everything we are.

We never lost them, and we can never lose them. We are them. We are the storm. In this dance, their lead is soft, nearly imperceptible, and often missed by a heavy follower. It is a lead that can only be felt when we quiet our minds and allow ourselves to listen to our own intuition.

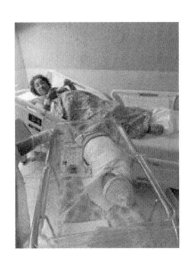

AFTERWARD:

HOW DREAMS COME TRUE

Knowing that I needed to continue, I did. Moment after moment. One foot in front of the other. Waking up to navigate babies, heartache, gratitude, and a farm project while trying to turn the house into a home and tend to the garden of my mind. Every day is a new day, but every moment stands alone and can be an opportunity to reset. This has been paramount throughout my grief to getting things accomplished and finding pockets of peace while navigating the unforgiving rapids of sorrow.

I didn't and don't try to stifle my emotions. If I needed to cry, I cried; it didn't matter where or in front of whom, but I also did the things I needed to do, and when the tears stopped, the moment was seized to change my focus. Seed by seed, transplant by transplant, lullaby by lullaby. I followed through with our dream of the house on the hill as my tears fell, building the farm as a permaculture project that works in harmony with the Earth; Infinity Farms, and raising our children as one with the land.

Because no matter what, time passes. It continues without prejudice. The rest of the world moves on as quickly as the next headline. Time is the only thing you truly have in this world, though borrowed and in surprise quantities. If you value something, you spend time on it. If you value someone, you spend time with them. The challenge for me was to start. I just needed to start. The storm raged outside, and it felt like a day to wait it out with a cup of tea and a movie in bed, but if I fall prey to that mindset... If I stay in bed, that's where the grief waits, hunting, claws extended, ready to pounce and overwhelm me until I remember that I need to pull myself out, seizing a moment as an opportunity to start again and change my thoughts, change my scenery, or make my heartbeat more quickly.

I planned. I drew out what I wanted to accomplish: where to plant papayas, eggplants, tomatoes, onions, potatoes, sweet potatoes, sweet peppers, lemongrass, lavender, mint, yucca, bananas, plantains, gandules, almonds, guava, guanabana, yerba buena, citronella, oregano, basil, thyme, oregano brujo, oranges, lemons, grapefruits, pineapples, ginger, turmeric, recao, kenaf, curry, anise, pennyroyal, neem, and moringa. I drew where I wanted the chickens and the goats. Where the horse would stay, and which areas would be sectioned off for grazing. I dreamed, I drew, and I made lists.

Then I started (If you miss this step, nothing will EVER get done).

Each day I worked and checked things off the list one by one because time passes no matter how you spend it. My children need our dream to come true. I need to live our dream or risk a withering soul.

I told myself that I would be happy again, but that's not true, because happiness hadn't left me. Looking at grief, you see the joy that was once and may be again with a simple perspective shift. Sometimes you can glimpse it in the eyes of the storyteller when she pauses and looks up with tears in her eyes. A moment of silence focused on a memory. A gentle smile. There was joy: it existed, or grief cannot exist.

You cannot lose someone who is part of you, but that takes moments of stillness to see. There was several moments a day, even in the worst of the worst, where I felt an intense appreciation, love, and gratitude for my son and daughter, even when I didn't feel it for breathing. I just had to allow myself to seek those moments out and feel them fully. I knew Alex didn't want to see me hurt as badly as I hurt. He fell in love with a happy, fun, adventurous me and stayed in love with a happy, fun, adventurous me. I also fell in love with the same happy, fun, adventurous, silly, energetic me.

Of course, he continued to want me to be happy, and more importantly, so did I. Imagine being so in love with somebody that you'd go out of your way to make them smile. You'd do anything for them. Make that person you. I made that person myself once again. I began to go out of my way to give myself reasons to smile beyond the beautiful children to whom I was waking up daily. I courted myself. Treating myself as someone I would work for, who deserved my love, patience, and understanding. I planted flowers everywhere so I could feel the awe of their radiance first thing each morning. I built myself a spiral heart Zen herb garden behind my kitchen that allows me to catch whiffs of beautiful scents throughout the day, and I kept plugging away daily at my delayed gratification. Our dream wasn't going to be something I would achieve overnight. Even as I write these words, I know that I haven't fully "arrived," but the reality is that the destination is death. There's no "arrival," and the sooner you learn that the sooner you realize that now is the only time that exists. Understanding that allows you to make more conscious choices for you. I am on a journey to accomplish the little tropical house on the hill with fruit trees by the door, living off the land, raising my children as ones with the Earth while being my own best friend, and dancing every chance I get. That's a process that will morph over the years. However, it looks, I am creating a home full of laughter and healthy, authentic living with my children who know and are reminded regularly that they were made in love. They are reminded to listen for their father's wisdom in the stillness of the rising Viequense sun.

I am running again. That makes me smile. Not 20 miles at a 7-minute pace or anything crazy anymore, but 3-8 miles at whatever pace I feel like running. It is my "puppy let out of the gate" moment each day. It took me a solid 9 years to be able to withstand the payment plan of pain from running regularly, but I've arrived. I'm there. I'm literally living on the land of my dreams, with the view of my dreams, and the white horse of my dreams. Finally, at the beginning of 2022, 5 years after moving to Vieques, I am teaching dance in El Centro de Bellas Artes. The dance studio of my dreams that was promoted to me in 2017 before Hurricane Maria swept in and changed everyone's plans. Dreams really do come true when you follow your intuition and take advantage of all opportunities presented that spark your soul, especially the ones disguised as work.

It is said that to be happy as an adult, you should do the same things you did as a child for fun. I ran at top speed, challenged my body, and revelled in the sounds of my own increased heart rate. I have regained the ability to do that again regularly. I created "choreographed" dances and skits for small groups to watch (sometimes just my dad). I have regained the ability to do that with my dance company. I even did it on a huge scale for my dance festivals. I wrote for hours on end without socializing. I still do. I looked forward to escaping into the "wilderness" in the rustic little fort that I made with Rosa. I've chosen to live there now. Rosa even assisted in the construction when she visited me, so it's basically the same, right? I read for hours as a child everywhere I went. These days, when I'm not writing, I'm reading in the evenings. I volunteered at the local Humane Society to be with dogs and train dogs. Now I have dogs, goats, and horses to train at home. I actively sought and continue to seek activities that speak to my soul to pass my time, even when my world has been exploding around me. *Especially* when my world has been exploding around me.

I understand deep in my being that these activities do not need to make sense to anyone else but me because they save me and have saved me. That is how I have found my peace. I aligned my thoughts, words, and actions and danced my way there as often as I could until I found myself dancing subconsciously. Dancing gracefully with the ability to watch myself kindly and support my progress through the process, just like a best friend would. Muscle memory through a ton of practice, with my mind. Because no matter what, time passes.

ABOUT THE AUTHOR

 Aurita Maldonado is a US Army veteran, Purple Heart recipient, and Afro Latin dance instructor who has danced intimately with Death.

She served more than 8 years in the military including two combat tours in Iraq and Afghanistan. After a 200lb IED exploded directly under her vehicle and three rounds hit her pack, she chose to simplify her life and follow her dreams.

She moved to Haines, Alaska to become a rafting guide in a bald eagle preserve and face her PTSD while running through the wilderness. In 2012, she contracted a severe case of rat lungworm which paralyzed her from the waist down, leaving her in a wheelchair with neuropathy over her entire body.

Aurita was told she wouldn't walk again, but they misjudged her determination. Her inspirational recovery is featured on Animal Planet's show: Monsters Inside Me: Season 5 Episode 1.

In 2017 Aurita moved to the 24-mile island of Vieques, Puerto Rico to teach salsa, but Hurricane Maria hit and shifted her focus to survival. She was pregnant with no electricity, water, nor communication. Her story was featured in the documentary, Broken Worlds: The Island (Vieques).

Her story was also featured in CNN Special Reports "Storm of Controversy: What Really Happened in Puerto Rico," hosted by Bill Weir, a year after Hurricane Maria.

Today she continues to reside in Vieques with her 2 children. She lost their father to a heart attack, but continued their dream and runs an organic farm, La Finca Infinidad. She is the director of Tropical Storm Dance Co. and teaches salsa, bachata, Zumba, and Latin Fusion Aerobics... All with a side of inspiration.

You can contact or connect with Aurita Maldonado at:
Instagram: @HurricaneInspired
Facebook: facebook.com/HurricaneRita2
Email: TheZenofDance@gmail.com